Endorsements

Can we really receive back from the Lord double for the trouble the enemy or the world or circumstances or our own choices brought upon us? In her latest book, Katherine Ruonala shouts "Yes," not only telling us it can be done but showing us the way. You do not have to live the rest of your life under the heavy weight of pain, guilt, regret, and disappointment. What satan meant for evil, God can use for good— greater good!

DR. MICHAEL L. BROWN
Host, *The Line of Fire* broadcast

From the first chapter, I could feel the manifest presence of God ministering to me as I read Katherine Ruonala's book, *Double for Your Trouble*. My faith soared as the words of truth flooded my heart and mind. Get ready to be lifted above the head of your enemy and live in triumphant faith and power. The thought that God gives us a divine exchange and restores double for everything life has tried to steal is 100% true! Being a full-time travel minister, I recently experienced this promised reality from God. A global pandemic shut down my travel ministry. I didn't know where our financial provision would come from. At the very onset God spoke to my heart that I would come out with DOUBLE. He spoke Job 42:10 to my heart and said I would come through with double provision. As I received His word and declared it over my life and ministry, we saw exactly DOUBLE come in divine provision. Katherine's book is filled with life, faith, and abundant glory. Read it and saturate your heart with every word contained in its pages. You will be transformed and will experience the divine exchange of goodness found only in Jesus.

MATT SORGER
Prophetic Minister
Author of *God's Unstoppable Breakthrough*
Podcast host of *Glory Living*
mattsorger.com

My friend, Katherine Ruonala, continues to bless me through her life and writing. *Double for Your Trouble* is a gift in a season of deep mourning after losing my spiritual father, Jack Taylor, after 21 years of daily connection. The good news of the gospel and this book is that Jesus came to redeem everything. He came to seek and save that which was lost (Luke 19:10). The thief comes to kill, steal, and destroy but Jesus came to give life and to give it to us abundantly (John 10:10).

This is a guide for anyone looking to find radical freedom, infectious joy, and authentic faith.

LEIF HETLAND
President of Global Mission Awareness
Author of *Healing The Orphan Spirit*

Katherine Ruonala's latest book *Double for Your Trouble* is a deep well of teaching, impartation, and refreshment. As I read through the pages I was overcome by the love of our beautiful Jesus and what is ours in Christ. What is available to us and purchased for us by His death and resurrection. I believe as you read through these pages you will be deeply ministered to by the Holy

Twitter
https://twitter.com/katherineruo

Instagram
https://www.instagram.com/katherineruonala/

Facebook
https://www.facebook.com/KatherineRuonalaMinistries

Ministry
http://www.katherineruonala.com

Church
http://www.glorycitychurch.com.au

Australian Prophetic Council:
http://www.australianpropheticcouncil.com.au

Contact details
Email: info@katherineruonala.com

Spirit. Many hearts will be healed, deep encounters with Jesus will take place as His words of truth fill your heart. Chains will break and a depth of revelation of your identity will flourish. The revelation of His love afresh will cause your heart to burn with adoration for Jesus like never before. Keys of wisdom and biblical principles are being handed to you in this powerful book for you to walk in greater realms of life in Christ. This book will change your life. This book is a gift and tool to put in your tool belt for this new era for you to walk victoriously in Christ.

LANA VAWSER

Lana Vawser Ministries

Author of *The Prophetic Voice of God, A Time to Selah, I Hear The Lord Say "New Era"*

My friend Katherine embodies the power of the message, *Double for Your Trouble*, otherwise known as believing God for double recompense. I have watched her boldly live a life of resolute faith, releasing miraculous breakthroughs for countless many. Katherine has written not just a guide for how to wage war with your promises, but a fiery anointed weapon that carries an impartation of faith to effect actual change. These words have been tried and proven true by Katherine, and will inspire hope, and empower you to claim your double blessing in the trenches of your life. As you put these powerful truths into practice, your life will be transformed. This is more than a book, it's a catalyst for blessing where you need it most.

JODIE HUGHES

Pour it Out Ministries

pouritout.org

Author of *The King's Decree*

Katherine is a precious gift from God for our generation. She is one of the most anointed ladies I know, and she moves powerfully in the prophetic and miraculous realm. So, this book is not just another book but it is God's heart for this season, as almost everybody from different nations and backgrounds has been shaken and experienced loss, tragedy, division, and pain. *Double for Your Trouble* is not a triumphalist declaration but is the expression of God's goodness and love for us that I've experienced in my own life after Katherine prophesied this over me.

Jean-Luc Trachsel
www.jeanluctrachsel.org
President of the International Association
of Healing Ministries (IAHM)
Prime visionary of Europe Shall Be Saved movement
Co-chair with Daniel Kolenda of the
Global Evangelist Alliance

The Apostle Paul promises that tribulation produces perseverance; and perseverance, experience; and experience, hope. If you have ever experienced tribulation, let Katherine Ruonala bring you the hope that you will receive a double portion and a double blessing for every trial you have faced. May *Double for Your Trouble* strengthen you and show you the promises that are yours.

Gordon Robertson
President, the Christian Broadcasting Network

More than a cute quip, Katherine's Ruonala's *Double for Your Trouble* packs a powerful punch in each chapter, equipping the reader with a virtual tool belt full of practical spiritual devices. I found the chapters delightfully easy to read, formidable in weight of content, and accessible in practicality and real-life application.

DAN McCOLLAM
Co-founder of Bethel School of the Prophets
and The Prophetic Company
Author of works including: *The Good Fight, Bending Time, God Vibrations, Finding Lost Things*

What a power-packed book—*Double for Your Trouble*! God's promises shine so brightly on every page of Katherine Ruonala's writings, especially this book! She makes the promises of God so accessible and real, no matter what you might be going through. Katherine writes from a deep well of devotion to Jesus and His Word, as she writes, "Scripture is an invitation waiting for a response." That says it all! The trouble you have experienced will be eclipsed by the promise that God makes to you —double blessing for all your trouble! Get this book and watch as your life changes in response to God's promises. Do you need a miracle in your family, your finances, your health? Learn how to access the power of miracles through each chapter of *Double for Your Trouble!*

BRIAN SIMMONS
Passion & Fire Ministries

Katherine Ruonala is an amazing woman, preacher/teacher. We have had her speak at some of our largest events. I am excited about her new book, *Double for Your Trouble*. We often don't find speakers talking about suffering, but suffering is part of life, and if we haven't experienced it yet, we probably will before we meet Jesus face to face. Katherine has given us a fresh look at redemptive suffering that may lead to redemptive victory. I recommend Katherine, her ministry, and *Double for Your Trouble*.

Blessings in and through Him,

Randy Clark, D.D., D.Min., Th.D.,
M.Div., B.S. Religious Studies
Overseer of the apostolic network of Global Awakening
President of Global Awakening Theological Seminary
amazon.com/author/randyclark
Skype ID randyrayclark

In First Samuel 30, when David and his men returned to Ziklag, they discovered that the Amalekites had raided the desert hill country. They had attacked Ziklag in David's absence, burned it, and carried away the women and all the other inhabitants who had remained behind. None of them were killed, but they were taken captive and carried off by the Amalekites. When they discovered this, they cried out and wept aloud until they could weep no more. David, too, was in anguish. Some of his men talked about stoning him because they were so bitter about their families being taken. What I love about this testimony of David is he encouraged himself in the Eternal One, his True God. This passage of scripture is an example for all of us when we come to a dark place in our lives where we feel robbed and hopeless. I believe these tests in life can be opportunities to change atmospheres and reverse curses through encouraging ourselves in HIM with thanksgiving and worship. David recovered everything that had been taken and brought everything home, even the Amalekites' wealth. I feel this experience with David is a "double for trouble" example that underpins the teachings in Katherine's new book *Double for Your Trouble*. This book will inspire you to be encouraged in the Lord when going through challenging times. This comes while meditating on God's specific promises.

This book has a lot of my favorite Scriptures where God promises to restore twice as much as His people have lost.

Many of us may feel vulnerable in these times of uncertainty. However, this book is a crucial read for the bride to overcome the enemy and shine with a double-portion blessing as a testimony of Jesus in this darkened world. I commend Katherine Ruonala for obeying this calling to write and inspire others.

ADAM F. THOMPSON
Prophetic ministry and international author
www.voiceoffireministries.org

Double for Your Trouble provides practical application to the biblical truth that God is able to take what the enemy meant for harm and turn it for your good. Katherine Ruonala's life exemplifies this beautifully, as she has partnered with these truths to see His promises fulfilled in her life. If you desire to learn how to remain in joy daily and live with hope for your future, this is the book for you.

SARAH CHEESMAN
Author and host of the *Happy Prophet Podcast*

DESTINY IMAGE BOOKS
BY KATHERINE RUONALA

Supernatural Freedom

DOUBLE

FOR YOUR

TROUBLE

LET GOD TURN YOUR MESS INTO A MIRACLE

KATHERINE RUONALA

DESTINY IMAGE® PUBLISHERS, INC.

P.O. Box 310, Shippensburg, PA 17257-0310

"Promoting Inspired Lives."

This book and all other Destiny Image and Destiny Image Fiction books are available at Christian bookstores and distributors worldwide.

For more information on foreign distributors, call 717-532-3040.

Reach us on the Internet: www.destinyimage.com.

ISBN 13 TP: 978-0-7684-5649-3
ISBN 13 eBook: 978-0-7684-5650-9
ISBN 13 HC: 978-0-7684-5652-3
ISBN 13 LP: 978-0-7684-5651-6

For Worldwide Distribution, Printed in the U.S.A.

1 2 3 4 5 6 7 8 / 25 24 23 22

Acknowledgments

Thanks to Emily Ruonala, Roslyn Mills, and Wendy Joyce for all your help in proofreading and editing. I love and appreciate you all.

Contents

Foreword *by James W. Goll* 1

Introduction 5

Chapter 1   The Principle of Restoration 9

Chapter 2   The Divine Exchange Table 29

Chapter 3   The Oil of Joy Instead of Mourning. 47

Chapter 4   The Greatest Exchange 63

Chapter 5   Encouraging Yourself in the Lord 79

Chapter 6   Partnering with God for His Promises. 95

Chapter 7   Waging War with Your Promises 113

Chapter 8   Dreaming with God. 133

Chapter 9   Mouths Open Wide 149

Chapter 10 Making Room for His Glory 169

Conclusion 187

Foreword

Years ago, there was an infamous song penned by an endearing, tender soul in extremely troubled times. The folk-style melody was permeated with resonating lyrics that conveyed a timeless message. *"I've looked at life from both sides now."* The song captured a generation. But did we ever really understand? I know for one, I tried, but I did not. Like many other sincere believers, I tended to live in the longest river in the body of Christ. It's called the River of Denial.

But God saved me from sugar-coated, superficial Christianity, and life baptized me into the fellowship of Christ's sufferings. After all, I had prayed like Paul, the apostle of old, that I might die to self and find my true identity, which is hidden in Christ Jesus. I prayed those dangerous prayers, like most of you, *"Not my will but thine be done!"* Problem is, He has a long, perfect memory and we tend to have a short, selective one!

When the Bottom Fell Out

I have lived a very blessed life full of incredible God encounters and mountaintop experiences, composed over 40 books, received international awards for achievements in various fields of endeavor, and have had the joy of being a father to four miraculous children and a growing number of grandchildren. But there was a prolonged period of time when the bottom fell out.

I walked through the valley of the shadow of death. I stared down non-Hodgkin's lymphoma cancer three times over a nine-year period and lost my best friend and wife, Michal Ann, to ravaging brutal colon cancer. As a result, I went $300,000 in medical debt, became a single dad, and became surrounded by Job's friends and was left to rebuild my life while living in a public goldfish bowl.

All the while, I had a relentless gift and calling from God that would not let me go, and I had the last word from my late wife that ordered me to *"Never, never, never give up!"*

So what's a guy supposed to do, anyway? Oh, I know, just throw in the towel. Right? Or is there another way to go?

The Power of CHOICE

Being created in the image and likeness of God, our Heavenly Father has given us a great gift. Want to know what it is? It is a free will. It is the power of choice! *"Choose this day whom you will serve."* I can choose to believe that something good is about to happen, or I can self-destruct by wallowing in the swamp of self-pity, victim mindset, and downward spiral.

Or I can flip the narrative on its head! I can lift my head off my chest and look up and raise my eyes unto the hills from whence comes my help! Yes, as delightful Lauren Daigle sings, *"Look up child!"*

I can choose to believe that my weakness is another divine opportunity where His grace is made strong! I can tell my heart to come alive and sing again and look for His promised rainbow to appear at the end of my storm.

Let us choose to believe that all things work together for good. Let us declare we have been called to God's purposes. Let us believe that the best is yet to come.

The Best is Yet to Come!

As my dear friend Katherine Ruonala aptly states, *"But God has not saved us for our hearts to be heavy. His promises don't leave us in a place of disappointment or despair. Our God has great plans and dreams in store for us."*

Sometimes my mind just does not get it. But my heart says, *"YES!"* We all lean one way or the other. So lean into God! Stop leaning into your limited, imperfect way of thinking. *"Trust in the Lord with all your heart and lean not on your own understanding."* Right?

That's when His redemptive plan kicks into gear, and He does exceedingly abundantly above all you can ask or think. That's when you get *Double for Your Trouble!* That's when your mess becomes God's next breeding ground for His next miracle!

That's the rainbow I'm still looking for. How about you?

With anticipation,

JAMES W. GOLL
Founder of God Encounters Ministries
Goll Ideation LLC

Introduction

I've come across a lot of people recently who are struggling with discouragement. Some are discouraged because of their current circumstances—perhaps a family situation, a financial or health issue, discontentment in their work, or any number of other disappointments or struggles. Some are weighed down by guilt and shame for the things they have done or wished they had done differently. Some are discouraged because of regrets and disappointments from the past or fears and anxieties about the future. And some are simply weary of well-doing.

Human minds tend to focus on whatever is going wrong, whatever needs to be fixed, and how life seems to be falling short of our hopes. As a result, many people, even strong Christian believers, are feeling heavy, confused, insecure, and anxious. They know God is on their side, but they are struggling to see Him through the clouds they think are hanging over them.

But God has not saved us for our hearts to be heavy. His promises don't leave us in a place of disappointment or despair. We were never designed to live with anxiety or fear. If we really knew His love and the plans and dreams He has in store for us, we would never be insecure. These thoughts and feelings are foreign to His kingdom.

So what can we do with all these feelings of regret, hurt, betrayal, disappointment, and loss? That's what this book is about. God gives us great and precious promises that address every one of our foreign thoughts and feelings. He has a solution for our guilt and shame, a remedy for every loss we've ever experienced, a comfort for every fear, an assurance for every insecurity, a healing touch for every regret, and a joy to offer in place of every sorrow. He is a master of restoration, and His Word is full of promises and prophecies that will restore our lives and fulfill our longings—*if* we know what to do with them.

So we're going to talk a bit about what these promises and prophecies are and what to do with them. We'll look especially closely at some of His specific promises for restoring us from the pain and shame virtually everyone has experienced at some point in their lives. And I think you'll be surprised at how extravagant and tender His words are—and at how accessible they are when you know how to apply them. I believe you'll be encouraged by the ways God intends to redeem every pain and loss, elevating you to a much better position than you ever thought possible.

The principle I had been thinking about for some time was the idea of double for our trouble—those verses in Scripture where God promises to restore twice as much as His people have lost, even when their losses were from their own disobedience or mistakes. He continues to give double recompense for wounds of the past, large or small, self-inflicted or caused by others. He loves to take our shame, pain, and disgrace and give us more in return. He does exceedingly abundantly beyond all we can ask or imagine.

This book is an invitation into that experience—not just as a theology or a theoretical idea, but in real-life application. Psalm 23 tells us that God makes us to lie down in green pastures and restores our soul. I think He wants us to experience that every day. He delights to lift up the weary. He is eager to heal wounds. He has made a way to pour out His goodness in much greater measure than we think we deserve. He wants us to know His presence, trust His promises, and apply them to our lives in some very specific ways.

As you read the pages to come, expect God to speak to you and refresh your soul. Open your heart and mind to the blessings He wants to give you in place of all your sorrow, regret, fears, insecurities, guilt, and shame. Take Him at His Word when He promises restoration that is far beyond what you have ever expected. Most of all, put these truths into practice. They have changed my life, and I am confident they will change yours too.

CHAPTER 1

The Principle of Restoration

Imagine having an extremely valuable insurance policy protecting everything you own. It not only guarantees reimbursement for the actual value of your possessions, it also promises much more to compensate for all the trouble you have to go through to replace whatever you've lost. In fact, it promises an upgrade—over and above everything you own. That's an amazing policy, isn't it? Not many companies are offering deals like that.

Then imagine that thieves break into your home one day when you aren't there and take all of your most valuable possessions. You come home to discover everything is missing—jewelry, electronics, even some sentimental items that you've held on to just because they are important to you. The pain of your losses is devastating. Your heart is broken.

What would happen if you never reported this theft to your wonderful insurance company? Nothing. You would simply continue to experience the pain of your loss. Over time, you might get used to having less and think all those blessings just weren't meant to last. Your wounded heart would remain wounded, and you might begin to assume that all good things come to an end. You would condition yourself to live with less satisfaction, less anticipation, and less hope.

If you want restoration in the broken places and lost opportunities of your life, you have to make a claim for it. Insurance companies don't come knocking at your door to see if anything is wrong. They don't pay their benefits if they don't know you've lost something. Even if they did know, there would be nothing they could do about it until you filed your claim. That's how it works. Restoration is not automatic. You have to know what to do to apply it to your life.

That's how God's promises work too. He knows about all your needs, of course, and He wants to heal and restore wherever you've experienced the shame, pain, and disgrace of losses and disappointments. But you have to claim His promises by faith in order to receive them. It doesn't do any good to complain to your family and friends that the insurance company didn't pay up or that God hasn't come through for you. You have to actually get up and believe, declare, and receive by faith what you've been promised.

I recently sensed the Holy Spirit leading me to pray very specifically over a proverb about thieves: "When he is found, he must restore sevenfold" (Prov. 6:31). The Holy Spirit challenged me over that verse and said He wanted to bring me the things that had been stolen from me. The enemy has stolen things, and I should claim restitution. The Lord told me I needed to be very intentional in bringing specific claims to Him so I could get back what the enemy has taken.

I've done that for years in general terms because so many of God's promises are about restoration. He wants to heal wounds, deliver captives, give sight to the blind, and repair broken lives. His Word is very clear about that. But this instruction from the Holy Spirit felt a little different. It was about going after these things much more specifically—remembering past moments of shame and loss and bringing them to Him for His forgiveness, healing, and restoration. In Jesus, I have the authority to insist that the thief make restitution, just like the proverb says.

So I've been doing that and applying it to areas of my own life like my relationships and my ministry, bringing it all to the just Judge who has cleansed me from all sin. I've always tried to keep short accounts with Him and receive His cleansing by faith, thanking Him for making me completely righteous through the blood of Jesus. I'm so grateful for that because it's done, it's thorough, and it's forever. But there's more. His Word says the thief has to pay back sevenfold whatever he has taken from me. It also gives extraordinary promises about God restoring our lives, which we'll look at in the coming pages. So I'm learning to bring all of those thefts to God, specifically naming them as I remember them, and celebrating the restoration that is coming.

Can you imagine what it's going to look like to have up to sevenfold return for the things that have been stolen from us in the past? I think about relationships that were sabotaged and how wonderful they are going to be when fully restored. I think about former shame, pain, and disgrace and get excited to think about how God will make it work out for my good. I've already experienced many of these blessings as I've brought the past back to God for His recompense, and it has been amazing. He's so good. Restoration is always on His heart for us.

The Promise of Double Recompense

Isaiah 61 is a beautiful passage about restoration—and not just a restoration of what was lost, but a double blessing in its place. For all the shame, pain, and disgrace we've experienced, He'll give us a double portion of His goodness. It's a passage Jesus quoted when He read the Scriptures at the synagogue in Nazareth because it speaks of Him and all that He was called to do. This is what those who are in Jesus get to walk in and experience.

> *The Spirit of the Lord God is upon Me,*
> *Because the Lord has anointed Me*
> *To preach good tidings to the poor;*
> *He has sent Me to heal the brokenhearted,*
> *To proclaim liberty to the captives,*
> *And the opening of the prison to those who are bound;*
> *To proclaim the acceptable year of the Lord*
> *And the day of vengeance of our God;*
> *To comfort all who mourn,*
> *To console those who mourn in Zion,*
> *To give them beauty for ashes,*
> *The oil of joy for mourning,*
> *The garment of praise for the spirit of heaviness;*
> *That they may be called trees of righteousness,*

The planting of the Lord, that He may be glorified.
…Instead of your shame you shall have double honor,
And instead of confusion they shall rejoice in their portion.
Therefore in their land they shall possess double;
Everlasting joy shall be theirs (Isaiah 61:1-3, 7).

The whole chapter is very powerful and encouraging, and I've only included portions of it here. It goes on to explain how the God who loves justice will bless His people and establish their reputation among the nations. He clothes us with garments of salvation and covers us with robes of righteousness, dressing us up the way a bride and groom adorn themselves for their wedding (Isa. 61:10). Wherever we've experienced ashes, He wants to give us beauty. Wherever we've experienced mourning, He wants to make us joyful. Wherever we feel heaviness, He wants to clothe us in a garment of praise. And He offers double honor and blessing for all the trouble we've gone through.

That's an amazing prophetic promise, isn't it? One of the most amazing things about it is that it was first given to people who were in trouble *as a result of their own sins and mistakes.* They had brought shame and disgrace upon themselves! However, God, in His great love for the Israelites, was already prophesying the blessing they would see on the other side of it. The ashes, mourning, and heaviness were their own fault, yet God was already planning to give them double honor and restore them with double blessing.

This promise of double blessing is echoed elsewhere in Scripture, sometimes even expanded. "Return to the stronghold, you prisoners of hope. Even today I declare that I will restore double to you," Zechariah prophesied to former exiles who had returned from captivity (Zech. 9:12). After all the troubles and losses Job experienced, God blessed him and restored to him twice as much in the end (Job 42:12-13). Joel prophesied that God would restore all the years the locusts had eaten (Joel 2:25). As we've seen, Proverbs commands thieves to pay sevenfold restitution (Prov. 6:31). Jesus told the disciples that anyone who left their homes, parents, brothers and sisters, and children for His sake would receive 100 times as much in this age and eternal life in the age to come (Mark 10:29-30).

Some of these promises are much bigger than double for our trouble. Whatever we have given up, suffered, or lost for the sake of the gospel will come back to us in one way or another, even in this life as we put our trust in God. These situations were each different, but the heart of God and His desire to bless us comes through in every one of them. He notices what we've been through, and He is not reluctant to give glorious, divine recompense for those who will believe Him for it. He promises extravagant blessings that are greater than our losses.

A lot of times we think we need to make ourselves righteous enough to qualify for God's promises. But that is impossible to do in our own strength. As the Scripture says in Romans 3:23, "for all have sinned and fall short of the glory of God." But, praise God, through Jesus we can be born again and receive the righteousness of God. We have been made righteous through faith in Jesus. He is our righteousness. We are the righteousness of God in Christ (2 Cor. 5:21). Whatever He stands to inherit, we inherit it with Him because we are His co-heirs (Rom. 8:17). It is no longer we who live but Christ who lives in us (Gal. 2:20). All of God's promises are "yes and amen" in Him (2 Cor. 1:20). We don't deserve these wonderful blessings, but He offers them freely to us. These promises are all fulfilled in Him, and as believers we are in Him. Therefore, they are ours to receive.

So God's heart for us is to give us a double blessing for what we've suffered. And whatever the thief has stolen from us is meant to be restored sevenfold. We can come to the Lord who makes beauty out of ashes because He is waiting for us to lay hold of His Word and receive what He wants to give. He wants us to apply our faith to these things in the same way we would file a claim with our insurance company—to point to the agreement and say, "Here, Lord, this is what You promised," and then believe that He is true to His Word.

The Importance of Taking the Next Step

We've had all of God's promises all along, but many people don't know exactly what to do with them. They are wonderful encouragements, but how do they actually apply to our lives? We read verses like Isaiah 61:7 and Zechariah 9:12 and want to connect with them, so we talk to God about them. Double recompense sounds so comforting. But until we actually come to Him in prayer and make a claim on these promises in faith, they may just continue to be encouraging and never become part of our experience. They are invitations awaiting our response.

One of my dear friends gave me a book, and I put it on my shelf and forgot about it. About a year later, I was going through a difficult situation and talking to her about it, and she quoted something from that book. *Ah,* I thought, *I should have read that.* So I picked it up and started reading it and realized it was one of the best books I had ever read. It had a been a great book all along, but it didn't do me any good just sitting on my shelf. It only benefited me when I began to use it.

God's Word is like that. It tells us everything we need pertaining to life and godliness (2 Pet. 1:3)—extraordinary and extravagant truths and promises that we can apply to every area of life—but it does us no good if we don't connect with it, pick it up, and use it. It's a little like having money in the bank but never accessing it. It's there. You have it in your account. You just don't enjoy the benefits.

James 2:26 is an interesting verse: "As the body without the spirit is dead, so faith without works is dead also." Many people have felt condemnation over this verse. But what James is saying here is that just as your body is alive because of the spirit that is within you, faith really only becomes alive when it is empowered by some word or act. However, we tend to look at it the other way around—that our faith empowers our actions—but James recognizes a spiritual truth that faith is just a mental belief until we start behaving as if our faith is true. Believing what the Bible says is powerful, but if we never apply it practically, we have missed the connection point of seeing its fruit in our lives.

God is not looking for us simply to be aware of His Word and agree with it. We can quote Scripture all day long, thanking Him that we're crucified with Jesus and He lives within us, reckoning ourselves dead to sin but alive to God in Christ, celebrating being a new creation, and rejoicing at how awesome it all is. That's great.

We should definitely do that. But if we don't actually take the next step and let what we believe work its way out, then we miss out on seeing it manifested in our lives.

So, for example, you can know that the Word says you are healed by Jesus' stripes (Isa. 53:5), but it must be claimed. Stand up and say, "Lord, that's what You said. I'm going to receive that. I want this applied to my life, and I'm claiming it by faith, believing You will do it." God's promises call for a response. Without that, you might get frustrated and wonder why they aren't working. He wants you to connect with them at every level of your thoughts and feelings and receive them by faith.

God wants us to be very deliberate about applying His Word to our lives. He actually wants us to wage war with the promises and prophetic words spoken over us. Those who know my story have heard me talk about doing this early on as my ministry began. When I was 23, God had promised that He was going to open doors into full-time ministry when I was 30. I had held on to that dream for seven years, but the year I turned 30 was a very discouraging year. It was really a difficult season of life. Nine days before I was to turn 31, it seemed like I was having fewer opportunities and doing less than ever. That promise looked hopeless and empty. There were no apparent prospects, and time was about to run out.

But I looked back through my journals and began to declare what God had said. I reminded Him of His promises and how I had been believing all these years that this was the time for doors to open. I fixed my gaze on Him: "Lord, there are only nine days left. You said You were going to do this. I'm thanking You for it now because You promised, and I know You keep Your promises. I'm making my claim for what You said."

That might seem a bit cheeky, but God loves faith. It pleases Him. When we come to Him like that, not as spoiled children but as people who believe He always tells the truth, He isn't offended at how demanding it sounds. He celebrates those who believe.

That's when my breakthrough came. I started to apply the Word to my life and get specific about it, and He spoke to me about going to a conference that had been on my heart. I got up and took the steps I needed to take to be there, and I ended up sitting next to a lady who turned out to be one of those open doors God had promised. She turned to me and said, "I feel like we should have lunch." Over lunch, she said the Holy Spirit was telling her to invite me to travel with her and be trained by her. God orchestrated the whole thing, and that's when opportunities began to open up into full-time ministry. He is very often waiting for us to act on the words, promises, prophecies, and dreams He has given us.

When we act on His promise for double recompense, we need to know the authority we have over the thief's works. We need to understand the basis for our faith. I was sick recently and thinking about going in for a checkup. As I was praying about that situation, I kept looking for the cause of it because I wanted to prevent it next time around. I heard the Lord say, "There is no cause."

I didn't understand that. "What do You mean?"

"A curse without a cause does not alight," He said (Prov. 26:2). "It can't find a place to rest. I want you to know that in you there is no cause. When you know there's no cause, you have the right to evict anything that comes on you illegally."

I thought that was very interesting. It makes sense. If a neighbor dumped a lot of trash in my yard, I'd have every right to tell him to move it. In the same way, I have the right to tell the enemy to go away and take his illegal curses with him. He still has a go at it, of course. He will do all kinds of things that are illegal, and we have the authority and the responsibility to pick up our weapons of warfare and go to battle with the Word of God. He says, "Many are the afflictions of the righteous, but the Lord delivers him out of them all" (Ps. 34:19). The trials and troubles will come, but we can trust God's deliverance every time. The weapons we have been given are mighty for pulling down strongholds (2 Cor. 10:4) and available for us to apply in any situation we need them, including experiencing God's double recompense in our lives.

I recently had a dream that highlighted this for me. In my dream, I was at a meeting when demons began to come in to attack people in the room. A really big demon came in and said, "I want Peter!" Then this big demon started coming after me. (I understood that Peter, in the dream, represented the leader or the spokesperson.) I tried to get away from this thing, but I was blocked every time and I began to despair of escaping it, as it seemed to block every effort I made to escape. Then, suddenly, I began to sing an old chorus.

> In the name of Jesus, in the name of Jesus, we have the victory.
> In the name of Jesus, in the name of Jesus, demons will have to flee.

When we stand on the name of Jesus, tell me who can
stand before,

In the mighty name of Jesus, we have the victory.

As I was singing, someone else locked arms with me, and we
marched out of the building as we sang. The demon was still there
but had shrunk in size and couldn't touch me or hinder me anymore. I realized that the Holy Spirit was reminding me to use the
name of Jesus as a weapon that I had been given to fight off the evil
attack. When I was trying in my own strength, I failed, but when
I used the name of Jesus, I gained the victory.

Like the name of Jesus, the Word of God is a weapon we can
wage war with. The promises in Isaiah 61 cover many people in
a lot of different situations—the poor, the brokenhearted, the
captives, those who mourn, those who feel weighed down, and
everyone under a burden of shame or confusion. That's a lot of
people. God assures us that we can get free from those conditions
and be doubly blessed instead.

The enemy would love to keep us in shame, pain, disgrace,
depression, discouragement, disappointment, and any other foreign currency that is not accepted in God's kingdom. He comes
to steal, kill, and destroy (John 10:10). That's his mission. But the
mission of Jesus is to destroy the works of the devil (1 John 3:8)
and give us abundant life (John 10:10). Anything in our lives that
is not life and light and abundance is from the evil one, and God
wants to replace that with all that is good and true and beautiful.

The Word tells us, "It is for freedom that Christ has set us free.
Stand firm, then, and do not let yourselves be burdened again by
a yoke of slavery" (Gal. 5:1 NIV). We don't need to try to figure

out why bad things are happening to us. "In this world you will have trouble. But take heart! I have overcome the world" (John 16:33 NIV). We simply need to recognize that it's illegal and say so. We go to the Word and say, "God, You said that I'm a co-heir with Jesus (Rom. 8:17). You said that no plague will come near my dwelling (Ps. 91:10). You said that by Your stripes I am healed (Isa. 53:5). Your Word says all my children will be taught by the Lord, and great shall be the peace of my children (Isa. 54:13)." That's just the beginning of His promises, a small sampling, the tip of the iceberg. You could go on and on.

If you see a circumstance that is contrary to the Word of God, you need to demolish the lie that would come against you, pick up the sword of the Spirit, and evict the enemy from his trespassing. That's what standing firm on God's Word looks like. That's the next step in contending for the double recompense He promised. It's like dealing with the rubbish that's been dumped in your front yard and deciding you're not going to tolerate it anymore.

The promise of double recompense, along with many others God has given us, means you no longer have to tolerate anything the enemy wants to dump on you. You don't have to put up with lies. You can exchange all of your foreign currency for the blessings of the kingdom.

Changing the Way You Pray

Many people spend too much time trying to figure things out. I know what that's like. I've had long, running conversations in my mind about the reasons for things happening and what I can do to prevent them next time. Not only do those mental conversations allow those problems to continue and work their way deeper into my life, they also occupy my mind with things that are not noble, just, pure, lovely, and of good report (Phil. 4:8). My mind should be full of wonderful thoughts about God and His kingdom, not about the things that don't look right.

If you're suffering with some kind of oppression or depression, try going straight to the heart of the matter. Recognize where it came from and send it back. You need to take the enemy to task with the Word of God and say, "No, that does not come from God! I belong to Him, and this is illegal. This is what the Word of the Lord says, and this is what we're going to do. In the name of Jesus Christ, I command that thing to go *now!*"

If you wake up and feel discouraged, don't just resort to telling everybody how discouraged you feel and fish around for someone to encourage you. People can help and encourage you, but God is the one who will give you victory. Ask the Holy Spirit where the discouragement is coming from. Recognize that it's a blanket of despair the enemy has placed on you. The kingdom of God is righteousness, peace, and joy in the Holy Spirit (Rom. 14:17), not discouragement and depression. Go ahead and lie down in green pastures with the Lord (Ps. 23:2). Talk to Him and let Him restore you. Let Him show you truth, and then whatever truth you receive from His mouth, pick it up and put it in your mouth. Speak it out. Expel the trespassers in the name of Jesus.

You can do that when you know what the truth is. You don't always have to figure out why; just figure out what the source is and then start declaring what you know to be true. You shall know the truth, and the truth shall make you free (John 8:32). But it only makes you free when you apply it.

When God speaks something to you—through Scripture, prophetic words, or the Holy Spirit's voice in your spirit—the next step (after believing it and receiving it, of course) is to speak it out. We'll go into more detail on that later, but it's important to know from the start.

I love it when God speaks to my heart. One of the reasons the Holy Spirit was given is to remind us of the words of Jesus (John 14:26). I'll sense Him reminding me of a word in Scripture, and that word becomes a *rhema* word, an in-the-moment truth I am meant to apply to a specific situation. It comes alive in a new way.

Receiving His Word this way is not just about knowing it and thinking it and then wondering why it isn't happening the way He said. We can know the whole Bible and still not experience it's promises. We have to take it in, and as He has spoken it out of His mouth, we begin to speak it out of ours. We need to deal with whatever is coming against us rather than waiting for someone else to do something about the situation. We speak His Word into our situations and cast out everything that doesn't fit His kingdom.

When we understand that, it changes the way we pray. Instead of believing like beggars, pleading with God to do something about the problem or asking Him why He isn't changing anything, we listen for His reminders. He helps us. He is eager to speak words of life and encouragement and abundance. But He wants us to do more than listen to His words of life. He wants us actually to do something with them.

God has already given us authority in Jesus. He has crushed the enemy under His feet and given us what we need to experience the same victory. Now it's our turn. He'll back us up, but we need to arise, shake off the dust, and go to battle with His Word. We can thank Him for His promises, rejoice and be glad in the day He has made, celebrate the promises He has given us, and get down to business with overcoming the enemy and receiving God's blessings.

Isaiah 35 is filled with promises similar to those of chapter 61. It's a beautiful passage:

> *The wilderness and the wasteland shall be glad for them,*
> *And the desert shall rejoice and blossom as the rose;*
> *It shall blossom abundantly and rejoice,*
> *Even with joy and singing.*
> *…They shall see the glory of the Lord,*
> *The excellency of our God.*
> *Strengthen the weak hands,*
> *And make firm the feeble knees.*
> *Say to those who are fearful-hearted,*
> *"Be strong, do not fear!*
> *Behold, your God will come with vengeance,*
> *With the recompense of God;*
> *He will come and save you"* (Isaiah 35:1-4).

Now that's a promise you can fight with. You can pick that up and say, "Lord, You said You're going to come with Your recompense and save. Thank You, Father. I'm expecting You to come with a vengeance. I'm believing and receiving Your recompense. I claim it, thank You for it, and ask to apply it to this specific situation. I hold it up to You as the agreement You established in Your own Word. This is my claim."

That's a powerful prayer because it is based specifically on what God Himself has said. It echoes that double recompense He promises in chapter 61. Together the promises on those Scriptures apply to all kinds of restoration—spiritual, physical, emotional, relational, and circumstantial healing. The deaf, blind, mute, lame, captive, brokenhearted, discouraged, and oppressed can all rejoice in their salvation and restoration. You can go ahead and celebrate the answer because God never fails to keep His promises.

Don't Give Up

A young boy who was born with a deformed head was once brought to John G. Lake. His deformity had put pressure on his brain and misshaped it. The boy was paralyzed on one side, had to walk on the side of his foot, and couldn't speak. His parents had taken him to their local pastor and asked him to pray, but the pastor told them healing miracles only happened in the time of Jesus and the apostles to prove His divinity. The boy's father said, "Well, I'd believe in the divinity of Jesus if He would do something for my son." But the pastor didn't have any encouragement for them.

Someone told these parents about John G. Lake's healing rooms, so they took their son for seven weeks to receive prayer. After praying every day for this boy, the family and the healing ministers noticed that he began to walk on the ball of his foot rather than on the side. So they kept praying and asking for more. His skull started to change shape, and after 13 weeks he had a completely normal-looking head. His speech fully returned, the paralysis was gone, and his parents enrolled him in a public school. When he was later interviewed, he was living a completely normal and healthy life and about to get married.

That's amazing! I was really challenged by that. We often give up when we don't see answers coming as quickly as we'd like. We just assume God isn't doing anything. But when we really believe the Word of God—not just theoretically or intellectually, but in the depths of our spirit—we know not to give up. We insist that even when we haven't seen any change yet, it must be coming because God promised.

That's the nature of faith. It's the substance of things hoped for and evidence of things not yet seen (Heb. 11:1). So many people seem to be confused about that. They think if they aren't seeing anything, faith must not be working. But faith, by definition, is based on what we don't yet see!

Abraham was rewarded for his confidence that God would do what He had said, even when His promise looked impossible. That's the kind of confidence God wants to release in us through the power of the Holy Spirit. In the book of Acts, the disciples were being challenged and persecuted, and when they gathered together with all the believers, they began to pray together. "Lord, look on their threats, and grant to Your servants that with all boldness they may speak Your word, by stretching out Your hand to heal, and that signs and wonders may be done through the name of Your holy Servant Jesus" (Acts 4:29-30). They didn't shrink back from their troubles and figure God must not have been with them. They pressed ahead. God looked at the boldness and the faith in their prayer and filled them with the Holy Spirit again.

God is waiting for glorious encounters with you like that. He wants the Holy Spirit to come upon you with power again and again. He wants to respond to the kind of faith that looks at impossibilities and says, "But I know what You said, Lord! I know who You are!" He's waiting for you to begin to posture your heart in expectation for His double recompense and His restoration of all that's lost, stolen, and broken in your life.

Then why doesn't He just come? Smith Wigglesworth used to say we shouldn't expect things just to fall on us like ripe cherries. He was urging people to really go after things they need with faith and expectation. He is looking for hearts that say, "Lord, I need this, and I know You want to give it to me"—and then *don't give up.*

I believe we can be filled again and again with the Holy Spirit, and He is waiting to be poured out into your life to overwhelm you with His love, stir up your faith, and motivate you to take steps toward the promises God has given you. F.F. Bosworth used to say that *faith begins where the will of God is known,* and restoration is something we know to be God's will. He has laid these promises out for us in His Word so we will go after them. He wants us to pray for restoration, for double recompense—for beauty instead of ashes, the oil of joy instead of mourning, and a garment of praise in place of a spirit of heaviness. He wants us to have the boldness to ask for and anticipate an outpouring of Himself into our spirits so that we overflow with all of His fullness and joy.

God is a rewarder of those who diligently seek Him (Heb. 11:6). We live in a culture of the instant—online information, drive-thru windows, fast-food delivery, ATMs, and microwaves—and many have virtually forgotten how to diligently and persistently seek anything or anyone. Many people just aren't interested if they can't get what they want immediately. We inherit the promises through faith and patience (Heb. 6:12). He's working His purposes, plans, and promises into every corner of our lives for the long term. We have to be persistent.

Sometimes we get excited when we sense the Holy Spirit for a moment, then walk out and forget the invitation that was included in that moment. God wants so much more for you. He wants to do exceedingly above all you can ask or think (Eph. 3:20). He wants you to posture your heart for the "more"—the double recompense, the full restoration, all the years the locusts have eaten, the beauty and dancing and praise in place of ashes and mourning and heaviness. He's so lovely and so kind, and His invitation stands, ready for your response.

Begin to open up your heart and say "yes" to the blessings He wants to give. Insist on the promises He has already put in writing and committed to fulfill on your behalf. The fullness of His promises is available to those who will get up, make a claim, and stand on that claim by faith.

CHAPTER 2

The Divine Exchange Table

As Tom and I travel around the world to many different countries, we have gotten used to exchanging currencies. Most countries conduct business only in their own currency, so if you want to buy anything with cash, you have to have whatever currency they use. But that currency isn't going to do you much good when you go back home or move on to another country. In fact, it just weighs down your purse or fills up your wallet. It's only useful in the places where that currency means something. So when we come back home from traveling abroad, we have to take our foreign currency to a place of exchange, hand it over, and receive back money we can actually use.

As citizens of the kingdom of God, we are meant to do business only in its currencies. But we come into the kingdom with a lot of foreign currency, and many people never go to the place of exchange to turn it in and receive back what they actually need.

The kingdom of God is righteousness, peace, and joy in the Holy Spirit (Rom. 14:17). There's no shame, pain, disgrace, heaviness, bitterness, sadness, rejection, or any other contrary spirit in the kingdom of heaven. That is all foreign currency to us. It does us no good in our kingdom citizenship. We don't have to walk in those things anymore. So whenever we recognize something that is foreign to righteousness, peace, and joy, we can bring it to the exchange table of heaven and receive the currency of the kingdom in its place.

Sowing Your Sorrows

As we saw in the last chapter, Scripture is an invitation waiting for a response. All the promises, prophecies, and purposes of God are invitations for us to accept and enter into. Knowing the Bible doesn't do us any good if we don't apply it. It's of no value. Knowledge alone puffs us up, but when we become doers of the Word, we get the benefits. We can then walk in freedom, righteousness, joy, and peace. Wisdom is vindicated not by its existence but by its deeds (Matt. 11:19).

Too many people look at the Word of God as a measure to compare and condemn themselves. Others look at it just as information and seem to think that knowing it is the same as believing it. That can be very deceptive. When we read or listen to God's Word and agree with it, that's wonderful, but that doesn't mean it is part of our lives yet. It's not just knowledge to store in our heads. It is the lamp to our feet and the light to our path. It's an invitation to step into the abundant life Jesus has called us to experience. So we have to read the amazing promises God gives us and actually do something with them.

With that in mind, let's look at Isaiah 61 again. It's a promise to Jesus—He quoted it when He read the Scripture at the synagogue in Nazareth (Luke 4)—but we are told that all of His promises are "yes and amen" for us too (2 Cor. 1:20), so these words apply to us. We are in Him, He is in us, and everything that He stands to inherit is ours too as His co-heirs. As He is, so are we in this world (1 John 4:17). So when Jesus opened the book at Nazareth to read about this extravagant and beautiful promise given to Him, He was also extending an invitation for us to enter in. This passage is about the Messiah, but it's also about our calling and purpose. We can say these things about ourselves.

That means that you are anointed to preach good news. Right now! You are not on a journey to become anointed and qualified to tell people the good news eventually. If you are born again— if you have received Christ as your Savior—you can already do that. He is anointed for it, and He is in you, so you are anointed for it through Him. In the same way, you are already qualified to receive beauty for ashes, the oil of joy in place of mourning, and a garment of praise in place of heaviness. These promises belong to Him and all who are in Him. There is nothing left to do but receive them by faith—to take your shame, pain, and disgrace to the divine exchange table and leave them there, receiving beauty, joy, and praise in their place. You no longer need to carry those things around with you. You only need to carry righteousness, peace, and joy in the Holy Spirit because that's what the kingdom currency looks like.

A religious mindset wants to stop right there and tell us not to go that far. "That's just a little too extravagant. We haven't earned that. We haven't become spiritual enough for *everything* God promises. We still have to grow in order to receive the fullness of the kingdom."

But is that what God's Word says? Doesn't it tell us just to see what God says and believe it? Yes, it's better than we deserve. Of course it is. That's always the way the blessings of God's kingdom work. His goodness and kindness are far greater than we feel like we deserve. That's why the righteous have to live by faith. If we live by analyzing and weighing the likelihood or the reasonableness of these things, we will talk ourselves out of them. If we were to live by our feelings or our merits, we would continually find ourselves not measuring up and spend far too much time condemning ourselves. But praise God, that's not how we receive the blessings of His kingdom. There is no condemnation for those who are in Christ. He came and set us free from the unreachable standard of God's righteousness by accomplishing it Himself. There is nothing to earn or deserve because Jesus already deserves it all. He gives it to us as a gift.

This means that even if you didn't measure up to the standard yesterday, you can still come to Him today and say, "Lord, here are my ashes. I give them to You." And He will be there saying, "Here, let Me give you My righteousness for that. I don't even remember your past sins. Here's My robe and My ring and My authority. You are the righteousness of God in Christ, and I give you My blessing."

That seems a bit rash, doesn't it? Why would God be willing to trust you with His authority right now, today, if you messed up only yesterday? Isn't that moving on a little too quickly? You don't feel qualified to lay hands on the sick, to pray with His authority, or even to receive His kindness so soon after messing up. How can He just give such amazing, undeserved blessings like that?

Praise God, even if our hearts condemn us, He is greater than our hearts (1 John 3:20). We can lay hold of the faith of Christ to believe what He says about us. His goodness is not dependent on our ups and downs. The righteous walk by faith. Anything less will cause us to miss the promises He has given us.

So we bring our foreign currency to the divine exchange table by faith. In faith, we sow our sorrows, our losses, our disappointments and regrets, our pain, and our shame as seeds into the soil of His kingdom, and in their place we see the fruit of righteousness, peace, and joy in the Holy Spirit. We release those things that are foreign to His kingdom, and He gives us kingdom currency instead.

We see an example of God's exchange rate in Isaiah 61:3. He has come "To console those who mourn in Zion, to give them beauty for ashes, the oil of joy for mourning, the garment of praise for the spirit of heaviness; that they may be called trees of righteousness, the planting of the Lord, that He may be glorified." We bring Him ashes, and He gives us beauty. We bring Him mourning, and He gives us the oil of joy. We bring Him heaviness, and He gives us a garment of praise in exchange.

But here's the catch: you actually have to exchange what you're bringing to Him. He doesn't give us a garment of praise to put over our heaviness or the oil of joy to apply to our mourning. He doesn't keep our ashes around but makes them beautiful. We have to give up the heaviness, mourning, and ashes—to turn them in and say goodbye to them. Beauty, joy, and praise are replacements, not cover-ups or add-ons. Jesus has borne our sorrows (Isa. 53:4) and invited us to cast our cares on Him (1 Pet. 5:7). We get rid of them and receive something much more precious in return.

So I come to God often and say, "Lord, I'm feeling a bit heavy here." Those moments of heaviness will come, and sometimes people walk around in that heaviness because they think they have to. If you're an intercessor or have prophetic gifts, you not only feel the heaviness of your own stuff; you can feel the weight other people's stuff too. But instead of walking around with it, it's important to learn to identify it. The moment you are able to recognize it, it's like finding foreign currency while a place of exchange is right there waiting for you. What are you going to do with that? You have a choice. You can sit there and let that valueless currency weigh you down, or you can get rid of it and get valuable currency in return.

I like how the Amplified Bible translates Isaiah 61:7:

> *Instead of your [former] shame you will have a double portion;*
> *And instead of humiliation your people will shout for joy over their portion.*
> *Therefore in their land they will possess double [what they had forfeited];*
> *Everlasting joy will be theirs.*

That's double for your trouble! We can bring God all our shame, pain, disgrace, or dishonor. We can itemize all our losses and disappointments. Anything that doesn't look like, taste like, smell like, sound like, or feel like the kingdom of God is foreign currency. Not only do we not have to live with it anymore, we can exchange it for double blessing in return.

Remember, this promise applies not just to the shame, pain, and disgrace that was inflicted on the people by others. It applies to everything they had forfeited—the trouble they had brought on themselves. Much of it was their fault. We have no business thinking, *I know God wants to restore what was stolen, but I did this to myself. I'm guilty.* The promise applies even to the losses, regrets, shame, dishonor, and mourning that we caused ourselves. It is God's delight to give us double recompense for our messes, regardless of who caused them, because He loves justice.

Is that actually justice? Most people pause right there and think, *Wait a minute. Justice is getting what you deserve. This is much better than I deserve.* But that's our own definition of justice. God's idea of justice is different. His way was for Jesus to live the righteousness we should have lived and take the punishment we deserved so He could lavish on us the goodness and kindness He has always wanted to give. It doesn't seem fair, but this isn't a question of fairness. It seems irresponsible, but God knows what He is doing. This is based on who He is, not on what we have done. He is smarter than we are. He knows that His goodness and kindness will lead to repentance. As He reveals His character to us and we recognize more and more who He really is, our hearts open up.

We are amazed by how good He is and have the opportunity to receive Him.

I sometimes forget to apply this principle. A situation that happened a few years ago came to mind recently, and I thought, *I haven't claimed that yet. I could take that and sow it for double recompense.* So often we think we just need to get over whatever has happened to us in the past. We're told that time heals all wounds. I don't know about you, but I don't want to carry around those scars. If someone has rejected you or you've been through a difficult situation, rather than just getting over it, why not bring it to the exchange table? "Lord, I thank You for double recompense there. Thank You, Jesus, that You not only make miracles out of messes but have provided a way for double blessing in place of all my sorrows." I can get really happy thinking about what that will look like.

I'm enjoying all the kingdom currency that has come into my life in exchange for my foreign currencies, and I'm quite excited about the overflow that is coming. I've stopped worrying about missed opportunities in the past and living with regret when all I have to do is ask God to restore what I've lost. I've learned that when people say nasty things about me online, there are much better ways of dealing with it than reacting the way I've often wanted to do. My instinct is to write back and try to explain my heart, but I have a husband who stops me if he finds out before I do that, and I've realized that my enemies don't want an explanation anyway. They just want to dishonor me. These are not opportunities for rebuttal, revenge, or regret. They are opportunities for blessing.

So instead of trying to defend myself, I take it to the exchange table: "Lord, that looks like dishonor in the media. It looks like I'm being shamed on the internet. This feels painful, so I'm going to sow that pain for double favor in the media and online. I'm going to have so much favor in exchange for that foreign currency. What the enemy meant for evil, You are going to use for my good. And Your exchange rate is absolutely magnificent. The enemy will regret that he ever did that because of the double recompense I get as a result. Hallelujah!"

And I have to tell you, that works! It's so powerful. God is so good and kind. His blessings are just wonderful.

Shaking Off Your Rejection

When Jesus was sending His disciples out on a mission to preach the kingdom of God and heal the sick, He gave them some very unusual and interesting instructions.

> *Now whatever city or town you enter, inquire who in it is worthy, and stay there till you go out. And when you go into a household, greet it. If the household is worthy, let your peace come upon it. But if it is not worthy, let your peace return to you. And whoever will not receive you nor hear your words, when you depart from that house or city, shake off the dust from your feet* (Matthew 10:11-14).

They were to go out and enter houses—to stay and build relationships—and take their peace into those households. In other words, they were not to go in all anxious and stressed out but to remember that God is their peace. We can do that too. I have to remember that I'm reckoning myself dead to sin and alive to God in Christ (Rom. 6:11) and thank Him that the Prince of Peace lives inside of me. I can be completely filled with peace and release it everywhere I go. So I practice that when I visit people's homes and even as I get to a hotel room when I'm traveling to preach. I say, "Lord, I let my peace come upon this room and this building." I want the atmosphere to be changed by what I carry. This is one of the ways God wants His people to spread His peace.

But then Jesus gave His disciples an instruction that sounds very odd to us—to shake the dust off their feet whenever a town did not accept them as a testimony against them. I've wondered about that passage because it doesn't seem very loving at all. It comes across as returning rejection for rejection, and that doesn't seem very much like Jesus' other teachings, like turning the other cheek, going an extra mile, or loving and praying for our enemies. But I think one of the things this verse is telling us is that when we experience rejection, we are not to carry it with us into the next situation or the next relationship. If we don't deal with rejection, that's what happens—it goes with us into our future relationships and affects them too. Instead, we are to shake it off.

That fits what we are told about the divine exchange table. You can shake rejection off and say, "No, I'm not going to carry that. That feels like pain and shame. Lord, I'm bringing it to You for an exchange. I'm not going to live in that rejection and carry the weight of it. I'm not going to live in the pain of that or remain in unforgiveness. I'm not going to hang on to that feeling and let it develop into bitterness. It's foreign currency, so I'm handing it over at Your exchange table for double recompense. Here it is. Thank You, Lord. The next place I go, I can expect to be fully accepted. I can expect to have favor with You and with people. I receive Your divine acceptance and trust that I will receive invitations and opportunities to replace that rejection, even at an accelerated pace." Then release that rejection to Him.

I'm a feeler, and rejection hits me in a pretty deep place. I feel it. I turn it over in my mind and let it create all kinds of turmoil in my heart, wondering why so-and-so doesn't love me, and thinking if they just knew my heart, they would love me like I think they should. But that can just go on and on, can't it? If I'm not careful, that can just weigh me down or hover around me like a bad smell. I even start to anticipate rejection from other people because it has been part of my experience. I carry it with me.

Can you relate to that? I think a lot of us handle rejection that way. It lingers and eats away at us if we let it. But God wants us to shake off every dust particle of rejection and refuse to let it cling to us. He wants us to hand it over at the exchange table and receive His blessing by faith, walk in His favor, and know how accepted and loved we are. That's what needs to linger in our hearts.

I was so encouraged by hearing my friend Kirrily Lowe speak recently on Isaiah 52. That chapter begins with a call to "Awake, awake!" I'm praying that the Holy Spirit will so wake us up and open our eyes to the truth of the gospel that we as a church will suddenly stop and realize, *Whoa, what was I thinking? How have I not seen all the opportunity and invitations God has given us?* I believe the Holy Spirit wants us to see the gospel with the eyes of a child who discovers amazing possibilities: *Did you know what this book says we can do? Are you aware of what it says we can have? This is amazing!* And I pray we would walk in all the miracles and opportunities the Bible says we can walk in. I see a coming awakening, just as this Scripture prophesies.

This verse goes on: "Awake, awake! Put on your strength, O Zion; put on your beautiful garments." In other words, we are no longer to walk around covered in shame, disgrace, and rejection. Then the next verse tells us, "Shake yourself from the dust, arise." The Hebrew word for *shake* is *na'ah*, and it carries the idea of a lion rustling his mane while he roars. I love that picture. It conveys the need to be vigilant in our rejection of things foreign to God's kingdom—to say, "No! In the name of Jesus, I will not tolerate that. I'm bringing it to the exchange table, I'll see in the face of God how loved and accepted I am, I'll receive His strength, and I'll drink deeply from the river of His pleasure over me." We are to shake the dust off vigorously like a lion who has had enough of it.

We can roar at the things that come against us, allow God's love to fill us up to overflowing—so much that we can hardly even handle it without His supernatural help—and then pray for the Holy Spirit to give us supernatural strength to receive even more so we overflow with the love of Christ for others. No particle of the dust of rejection can cling to us with that. Its smell is overcome with the fragrance of Christ. The difficult situations that brought us down become the very situations that lift us up because we bring them to the exchange table and receive double recompense in return.

The good news of the gospel is that hope in God does not disappoint. The exchange table is not a place for wishful thinking, the kind of hopefulness that just makes us feel better. That's not what biblical hope is. Biblical hope is a certainty of the good that is coming. This is an actual exchange, and we can anticipate the currency of the kingdom in return. That's a promise from God.

Psalm 37:3 tells us to feed on God's faithfulness. Revelation 19:11 tells us that "Faithful and True" is written on the thigh of Jesus. It's His name. God promised that He would give us double recompense for our former shame, pain, and disgrace. Because He is faithful and true, there is no room left for our doubts and questioning. There is no looking for the fine print or the hidden conditions. We come to Him with nothing but gratitude for working all things together for our good, as He promised (Rom. 8:28).

"All things" includes our shame, pain, and disgrace. So we come thanking Him, not asking if He might be willing to help us out this time, but trusting that He is eager to save and restore. He has borne our sorrows, invited us to cast our cares on Him, and told us to shake off the dust of rejection like a roaring lion shakes his mane. We have no reason to live in the dust of the past. We simply sow it into the soil of the kingdom and receive the double blessing that comes from it.

Isaiah 52 then goes on to say, "Loose yourself from the bonds of your neck, O captive daughter of Zion!" The lies we agree with can very quickly become shackles around our necks. The enemy tries to enter into our wounds of rejection and shame and say, "See there? You aren't loveable. You're... (selfish, bad, lacking in integrity, alone, or a myriad of other lies you can fill in the blank with)." As soon as we agree with that lie, it becomes a bond around our neck. The Lord is telling us in this verse to loose those bonds. He doesn't say He is coming to loose them for us. He has already done everything we need Him to do to break free of them. It's time to loose ourselves.

How do we do that? By shaking off the lies and bringing in the truth in their place. By roaring like the lion. We come in with the Word of God and say, "Lord, You said You would give me beauty instead of ashes. You said joy and praise instead of mourning and heaviness. You said I could hand over my pain, shame, and disgrace, so I'm giving it all to You. I'm not going to have it anymore. I want Your double recompense in exchange." And then we choose to walk in faith believing we've received it.

Tearing Down the Lies

What have you been believing that doesn't line up with the truth of what God says? Any thought you have about yourself that doesn't line up with what He says is a lie, and we are told to take captive every thought that exalts itself against the knowledge of Christ. So whenever you look at your future with discouragement, that thought needs to come down and be replaced with the truth—God's promise to prosper you and give you a hope and a future (Jer. 29:11). Whenever you think of yourself as stupid or unworthy because of a mistake you made, you need to realign your thoughts with the knowledge of Christ, who calls you holy and beloved. Remember, "as He is, so are we in this world" (1 John 4:17), so you look like Him. You may not see yourself that way, but He sees you that way. Tear down the lie, cast it away, take hold of the truth, and thank Him for what He has said about you and His plans for you.

I once talked with a man who had come up to the altar who said he had been told all his life that he was a naughty boy. He was a grown man and a believer in Jesus when he talked with me, but he still carried that label, which was placed on him at a young age. He couldn't get past this deeply held belief that he was bad. He started crying and saying, "I'm not a good person. I'm just not a good person." So we talked for a bit. I asked him if he had given his life to Christ, and he said he had. I asked if he had repented of and turned from his sin and received Christ's forgiveness in exchange, and he said he had. So I explained that if God's Word says he has been cleansed, forgiven, and made pure and holy in God's eyes, he was clearly believing a lie.

We spent some time pulling down that stronghold and exposing the lie. I assured him of the truth—that he was not a naughty boy and not a bad person. He was holy and beloved, purified and adored by the Father who declared him to be righteous in Christ. I told him, "God looks at you and says, 'You are as anointed as Jesus is. The same works He did when He walked the earth, greater works will you do. This is the truth about you. When I look at you, I see My Son. I see holiness and righteousness. You aren't just covered with the righteousness of Christ. I see you as one who is transformed and has become righteous. Your crookedness has been taken away. This is who you are.'"

It's very easy to define ourselves by what we've done, but that would be self-righteousness—a standard of righteousness that is based on ourselves. When we define ourselves by our own works, we become either self-righteous or self-condemning. But praise God, we are not defined by what we've done. We are defined by what we believe. We lay hold of the righteousness of Jesus by faith. He is our identity. We clothe ourselves in Him and the beautiful garments He gives us—the superpowers of compassion, kindness, humility, mercy, and so much more. We don't try to achieve these things. We pick them up and wear them because God said He gives us the garments of salvation (Isa. 61:10). He gives us everything pertaining to life and godliness (2 Pet. 1:3). We simply look at Him and remind ourselves of what we look like.

That's how we grow as believers—not by trying harder but by seeing who we really are. We have been made to look like Jesus, and He is love. Love is patient and kind, so we are patient and kind. We can pick up that invitation and walk in patience and kindness today, not one day when we eventually grow into it. We are clothed supernaturally in all the attributes of love because that's who God is. We wear the peace that passes understanding. No matter what's going on around us, we don't have to be stressed out and frustrated, carrying around fears and anxieties. That's not who we are anymore. We receive in exchange for all those things a garment of praise. We receive the peace of Christ. We don't try to be new. We just are.

The divine exchange table is the key to living the life God has called us to live. Too many believers live below His best for them because they haven't understood that their lives are no longer a matter of measuring up. They don't realize that they have access to all the treasures of God. We don't have to become qualified for anything. He has already qualified us. He has not called us to live with the weight and heaviness of stress, fear, anxiety, discouragement, regret, shame, and dishonor. He has not placed on us a robe of sadness and sorrow. He invites us to give Him the pain, the heaviness, the shame, and everything else that weighs us down and exchange it for the beautiful, wonderful blessings of double recompense.

CHAPTER 3

The Oil of Joy Instead of Mourning

When I was ministering in South Korea recently, I met a man who had a Ph.D. in laughter. He had researched and participated in studies that show that laughter, even when it's just simulated (i.e., laughing when you don't feel like laughing), has wildly wonderful health benefits. It boosts immunity, increases longevity, decreases stress hormones, decreases pain, triggers the release of the endorphins that promote an overall sense of wellbeing, increases blood flow and the function of blood vessels, protects against cardiovascular problems, improves mental health, eases anxiety and tension, and therefore increases resistance to all sorts of diseases. It even burns calories. According to a study in Norway, people with a strong sense of humor tend to outlive those who don't laugh as much. It adds joy and zest to life and improves our mood. It's a really good thing.

All of these amazing effects of laughter have been scientifically proven, and this man had made a career out of this field of study. He was employed by a hospital system to work with cancer patients, because laughing greatly increases their chance of recovery. At the end of every meeting or phone call with a patient, he tells them, "Okay, we're going to laugh for 90 seconds now." That's the optimal amount of time where the benefits really start to kick in. So he and his patients simulate laughter for 90 seconds as part of their therapy.

This doctor is a believer, so he knows what the Bible says about the benefits of laughter and speaks to audiences about a merry heart being like medicine, the joy of the Lord being our strength, and the kingdom of God consisting of righteousness, peace, and joy in the Holy Spirit. The Korean Christians he speaks to have responded so well to that message, agreeing with all the scientific data and the scriptural basis, and they laugh right along with him at the end of his messages. He spoke at the conference I was in, and when it came time for the laughing at the end, my daughter Emily and I felt a little awkward standing there while everyone around us was laughing on purpose. But soon we joined right in, and it felt really good!

I've put that practice to the test in a few difficult situations lately. I was driving home one night at the end of a long day, and these situations and the people involved in them kept coming to mind. I was tired, and I wasn't resisting negative thoughts very well. I felt the emotions of everything that was going on, and I think I felt the emotions of some of the other people involved as well as my own. I realized I was carrying all of this heaviness inside, so I started bringing it to the Lord, lifting it up to the exchange table, and thanking Him for what He was going to do in response. And then it occurred to me to start laughing like we had done in Korea. So right there in the car, really tired, a bit stressed, but realizing no one could hear me, I started laughing out loud. And it felt wonderful. The heaviness lifted. Laughter really was like a good medicine in that moment, and it changed my entire perspective.

Rejoice—and See Breakthrough

I think we can see that dynamic in Isaiah 54, which gives down-and-out people some really unusual instructions:

> *"Sing, O barren,*
> *You who have not borne!*
> *Break forth into singing, and cry aloud,*
> *You who have not labored with child!*
> *For more are the children of the desolate*
> *Than the children of the married woman," says the*
> *Lord.*
> *"Enlarge the place of your tent,*
> *And let them stretch out the curtains of your dwellings;*
> *Do not spare;*
> *Lengthen your cords,*
> *And strengthen your stakes.*
> *For you shall expand to the right and to the left,*
> *And your descendants will inherit the nations,*
> *And make the desolate cities inhabited.*
> *Do not fear, for you will not be ashamed;*

Neither be disgraced, for you will not be put to shame;
For you will forget the shame of your youth,
And will not remember the reproach of your widowhood
anymore.
For your Maker is your husband,
The Lord of hosts is His name;
And your Redeemer is the Holy One of Israel;
He is called the God of the whole earth.
For the Lord has called you
Like a woman forsaken and grieved in spirit,
Like a youthful wife when you were refused,"
Says your God (Isaiah 54:1-6).

This is quite an amazing and encouraging passage. The whole chapter goes on to give promises about God's protection, His commitment to teach our children, and the futility of any weapon raised against us. But it begins with people who have been ashamed—the "barren," those who have not seen the birthing of what they desired, who have been disappointed again and again, and who have been pushed aside for being unfruitful.

God speaks to these people and tells them to sing. It's a very strange command, isn't it? They are not in a situation that would naturally prompt any singing or rejoicing. They are living in disappointment. But He tells them to be exceedingly joyful. Why? Because He wants them to start rejoicing in faith about what they haven't yet seen. It's the same instruction Paul gives to the Philippians: "Rejoice in the Lord always. Again I will say, rejoice!"

(Phil. 4:4). God is looking for people who will be intentional about their joy.

Joy is not something that just happens to us. It's a choice we make. And sometimes we have to make that choice entirely by faith in the God who has promised something we don't yet see. That kind of joy expresses extreme confidence that the One who has promised will bring it about (1 Thess. 5:24; Ps. 57:2). He is faithful, and when we start to celebrate, dance, and get happy about His promises, we see breakthrough come.

Some dear friends of mine work in a country that is closed to the gospel. I went to visit them, and on the day I arrived, they were planning to bring their passports to meet me at the border and take me across. But that morning, they couldn't find the wife's passport anywhere. They looked all around, and the time was getting close for them to come meet me, but they couldn't do it without their passports. They were in a real bind.

They began ringing up friends and family members to ask them to pray. And when they still couldn't find it, they decided that maybe they should dance. So they began to jump up and down, dance, and celebrate with joy the fact that God had given them what they asked for. *We've asked Him to show us where this passport is,* they thought, *so let's celebrate the fact that we will be able to go and pick Katherine up.* They thanked God, cheered, and talked about how wonderful it all was, right there in the bedroom by themselves. They got really happy about it, dancing for joy over the fact that they had found the passport, even though they still had no idea where it was.

While they were singing, the husband's mother rang back and said, "The Lord told me it's in a box underneath your bed." So the couple looked under the bed, found the box, looked inside, and there was the passport!

Sounds crazy, doesn't it? Some people might look at that and think it's pure lunacy. But you can decide that either something like that is crazy and not bother with it, or you can rejoice and see breakthrough. You can go ahead and be crazy and see what happens, or you can just miss out on the good things God has in store for you. They made a choice to rejoice, and that celebration brought the breakthrough they were looking for.

David gives us a good example of that. Many are familiar with Psalm 27, where he says, "One thing I have desired of the Lord, that will I seek: that I may dwell in the house of the Lord all the days of my life, to behold the beauty of the Lord, and to inquire in His temple" (Ps. 27:4). But a lot of people read that without stopping to think that the temple didn't exist yet. God told David it would only happen in the next generation, with David's son Solomon. Still, David set his eyes on it, wrote a psalm for its dedication (Ps. 30), took up offerings for it, gathered materials, made up blueprints, had people pray over it, and praised God for it (2 Chron. 29). And after talking about this deep desire that had not yet been fulfilled, he ended Psalm 27 on a very positive note: he believed he "would see the goodness of the Lord in the land of the living" (Ps. 27:13). In other words, he refused to live in disappointment. Like the barren in Isaiah 54, he began to sing.

God is inviting us into that kind of partnership. I believe He is telling us in this season that one of the ways we will see the fulfillment of our promises in the coming days and years is to start rejoicing in faith about what we aren't yet seeing, believing it's going to come to pass. We can get all distressed and depressed about the disappointments we see, or we can trust that the answers are coming and rejoice over them. That's a choice. But getting distressed and depressed is not the way to partner with God because He never feels discouraged about anything. We partner with Him by making the choice to celebrate His answers. When God says to "sing, O barren," He's calling for an intentional joy and celebration about what we have not yet seen.

Worship—the Response of Faith

When Jesus was talking with the woman at the well in John 4, He said that the Father was looking for people who would worship Him in spirit and in truth. In other words, He is looking for people who respond to truth in such a way that it provokes true worship—not simulated worship, as we can do with laughter, but real, heartfelt responses.

A true, heartfelt response is not just an emotion. It's a choice to respond to a revelation about Jesus. When the Holy Spirit reveals to us a truth about who Jesus is, He wants that revelation to do something in our hearts—for us to say, "Yes, Lord, You are worthy of praise, and I'm going to give You honor and glory." It's a conviction that provokes a genuine, heartfelt response to who Jesus is. That's the substance of true worship.

When I was a teenager, I'd walk places to save bus money, often uphill carrying my backpack or whichever instrument I was learning at the time. I would make up songs and sing them while I walked. One of the first little songs I ever wrote—just for me, not with any intention of performing or publishing—was about God's patience. "Your patience abounds, O Lord, Your love, it knows no end…" I'd go on and on, and then I'd talk to Him, telling Him I just wanted to be His servant and live only for Him. What was happening there? That was a heart response to thinking about how patient God is. I loved His patience, and it drew out of me a desire to love and serve Him. That's what heartfelt worship is. Revelation about the nature and character of God always invites or provokes a response in us.

God is looking for us to focus on who He is, thank Him for His faithfulness and His character, and allow a response to come out of our hearts based on what we have recognized in Him. This is often a spontaneous process, but He wants it to be more than that. He wants us to be intentional about celebrating who He is.

When we are able to see and celebrate His nature and character, all of His lovely attributes, our hearts are much more prepared to rejoice and sing about what we haven't yet seen. That's easy to do when we've been worshiping Him for His faithfulness. If He is called "Faithful and True"—if that's so foundational to His nature that it's a name written on His thigh (Rev. 19:11)—our doubts and suspicions about His promises are undone. We focus on His utter and complete reliability, and that provokes a celebration in our hearts. We let our hearts dwell on the fact that He is faithful, He's made us co-heirs with Christ, His promises are "yes and amen," He is the God who cannot lie, and His Word is truth. These are all scriptural statements about His faithfulness that should be resonating in our hearts. The only appropriate response to His faithfulness is to get happy about it. His promises are wonderfully, irrevocably, perfectly true.

When the Holy Spirit reveals that truth and it begins to sink into our hearts, we can make a deliberate choice to rejoice, dance, celebrate, sing, and shout "hallelujah!" In our church, we sing songs about fighting our battles with worship. What we're declaring in song is that we will militantly sing and celebrate the things we have not yet seen come to pass because our warfare of worship is making a way. It's leading to breakthrough. We are insisting that God's faithfulness will prove true in the end and that all of His promises will be fulfilled in our lives. By faith, we are casting our worship forward into that time when we will see increased favor, double recompense, the oil of joy and the garment of praise, and all the blessings that have come to us at the divine exchange table already in our hands. We are choosing to live in the experience of the still-yet-to-come. We may not be there on the timeline yet, but those experiences are certain because our faithful God's promises are unquestionably true. That's worth a huge celebration, lots of dancing, and loud rejoicing and praise!

I had my first baby when I was still a very young married woman, 23 years old. I stopped working in order to stay home and take care of her, and then our other children later. But while I was home, I was so hungry for God, so desperate for more of Him. I wanted to see miracles, walk in His anointing, and pray with power. I loved Him with so much passion, and while the babies were asleep, I'd be on the floor praying.

One day I prayed, "God, I want to learn how to do intercession. But I don't know what it's supposed to look like. I don't know what I'm supposed to bind and loose. I don't know what to yell at or what to command." I had seen people praying that way and getting involved in "spiritual warfare"; I just didn't have a picture for how it all worked. "Lord, how do I fight spiritual battles? How do I pray like a warrior?"

I heard the Lord say, "Worship Me. When you start worshiping, everything shifts." That's where it all starts.

When Jerusalem was once surrounded by hostile armies, King Jehoshaphat turned his attention to God. He acknowledged God's nature and character, talked about His faithfulness and power to save, and then said: "We have no power against this great multitude that is coming against us; nor do we know what to do, but our eyes are upon You" (2 Chron. 20:12). He focused in the right direction.

God responded through the words of a prophetic voice and gave His people a promise. They could put their fear behind them because they would see the Lord's salvation. They wouldn't even have to fight; they only needed to position themselves and stand still (2 Chron. 20:17). So Jehoshaphat appointed the worshipers to go out first to the battlefield. As far as we can tell from the passage, God didn't instruct him to do that; it was just his grateful response to the promise. As the worshipers went out, they sang: "Praise the Lord, for His mercy endures forever" (2 Chron. 20:21). That's when breakthrough came—when worship was a heart response to God's character and His promises. Both armies set ambushes against each other, but the people of Judah never had to lift a weapon to win that victory.

Worshipers make a way in warfare that supernaturally causes victory to come. Why would Jehoshaphat send singers and tambourines out in front of the army to face an enemy holding swords and spears? It seems to make no sense. It's a lot like walking around the walls of Jericho, which must have seemed pointless to the Israelites entering into the Promised Land—until the walls fell. Sending out the worshipers like Jehoshaphat did wasn't and has never been a common military tactic. It puts your most vulnerable front forward, at least from a military perspective. But if God is your Warrior, inviting Him into the battle seems to be a really sensible thing to do. He is your first and only line of defense.

When you start to worship God, you are partnering with heaven by faith. Faith is released when you make a choice to worship, celebrate, and rejoice.

That's what happened with Paul and Silas too. They were in prison in Philippi because they had been at the center of a riot, and all they had done was cast an evil spirit out of a servant girl. Her masters didn't like this; she could no longer be a fortune-teller, and they could no longer profit off of her. So they stirred up a crowd, and Paul and Silas were brutally beaten and locked in iron shackles and chains that were designed not only to keep prisoners in place, but also to increase their pain.

What did Paul and Silas do? Instead of howling and moaning, complaining about the unfairness of it all, strategizing ways to get a message to someone or figuring out a way of escape, they decided to worship. They sang songs of joy and praise. They were loud about it too. Other prisoners were listening and probably really confused by what they heard. Suddenly there was an earthquake, their chains fell off, the doors flew open. The jailer started to panic because he was afraid prisoners were escaping, and Paul told him not to harm himself because everyone was still there. Paul and Silas then led the jailer and his family to Christ.

God turned their situation completely around in response to their heartfelt worship. They were in a dismal position and ended up with a glorious outcome. The authorities actually had to come and apologize to them for mistreating them. It was a remarkable victory. That's what can happen in the warfare of worship.

It's Time to Start Laughing

God wants us to recognize that His ways are not our ways and His thoughts are higher than our thoughts. He is looking for those who will be really intentional in their rejoicing, celebrating His promises with childlike faith. Faith that worships God before you've ever seen a hint of the answer, that rejoices in His promises even when you haven't experienced the outcome yet, that sees worship as a first resort rather than an after-the-fact response, is the kind of faith that brings breakthrough. Things shift.

Worship is powerful, but it's not just a tool or a key to get what we want. It's a heartfelt response to who God is. We know that; if you've been a Christian for any length of time and read the Bible, you've seen the priority of worship. But God wants us to go beyond knowing into actually applying. He wants us to be able to celebrate Him in our everyday situations.

People who work with me know that my "hallelujahs" have increased over the last few years. My innate response to almost every situation—good, bad, or ugly—is "hallelujah, praise the

Lord!" I have trained myself to be intentional about it because I know that whatever the situation looks like, God has a plan to work it out for my good because I am among those who love Him and are called according to His purpose (Rom. 8:28). So when a difficult situation comes up, I say "hallelujah." There is going to be something good in it. I will get double recompense for every pain, shame, and disgrace, every loss and disappointment that I sow into God's kingdom at His exchange table. That's worth celebrating.

Some people may think this "hallelujah" response is just a trite little expression, but it isn't for me. I believe God wants that praise to become an automatic response in the hearts of His people—not because we are trying to cover up our pain or be religious, but because we know in our hearts who He is and what He has promised. We come to know Him as the faithful God who gives us double for our trouble, so the trouble no longer bothers us like it once did. We know it's going to work out for our good.

When we know this, all our pain and losses become keys to a place of blessing. We need to learn not to waste any of it. Anything we have ever lost, any heartache we have experienced, any shame we have carried around with us can all be more than compensated for by the restoration God promises. I've watched it happen. God doesn't forget these things we've experienced. I've received double honor in places where I've been dishonored. Even people who have spoken against me have later come to work with me. If you will allow Him to watch over His promises and fulfill them in your life—and if you will learn to laugh, sing, celebrate as though it has already happened—He will come in such magnificent ways that you will have no heartfelt response other than deep, grateful worship.

Remember, none of this happens because we have earned, deserved, or matured our way into receiving His recompense. He gives it because He loves us. He delights in us, and He wants us to delight in Him with overflowing joy. He wants us to rest in Him and enjoy the glory that is coming. When we do—when the barren have learned to sing—we enter into a fruitfulness we've never before experienced. He is so wonderfully, amazingly generous and kind that He gives us double for our trouble and often much, much more.

When we get deliberate about our heart responses, we can recognize God's goodness in the midst of any situation. We can say, "Lord, this problem looks a lot like shame, pain, and disgrace, so I'm just going to bring that to You. This is actually an excellent position to be in. It's going to be good because You said I can have double recompense. I'm going to get a double blessing. Hallelujah!"

Can you imagine how different your life would be if that became your default posture? Imagine having a need—and dancing, celebrating, singing, and rejoicing about the answer before it ever comes, like my friends did when they couldn't find the passport. We can count on the fact that no weapon formed against us will prosper—that's the promise given at the end of Isaiah 54. We can go ahead and count on God working things out, and whatever He works out ends up being glorious.

The enemy doesn't like that kind of faith. He'll say all sorts of things to convince you that you are in a terrible spot. "This is miserable, here's what's going to happen, this is not going to turn out well." Those kinds of whispers may bounce around in our heads all the time, but they aren't from God. Psalm 2:4 says the Lord sits in heaven and laughs at those plotting to do evil. He knows it's going to backfire. He laughs at their plans. They won't get away with it; God will either prevent them from carrying out their plans or turn them into blessing for His people. He can already see the glorious end.

The laugh of the Father is inside of us just waiting to come out whenever difficult circumstances arise. When threats come our way, we can say "no" to fear and laugh at the presumption behind whatever the enemy wants to do. The Father wants us to engage with Him in the joy He already has. He already knows the outcome, and whether we know it or not, we can trust that He's already worked it out. He makes all things work together for our good.

It's time to start laughing. Fake it if you have to, at least when you start. I promise it will catch on. It will feel good. The joy of the Lord will rise up within you and become your strength. The celebration of His promises will break through and shift the bonds around your neck. The heaviness will lift, the mourning will turn into dancing, and the ashes will be replaced with something beautiful.

Sing, O barren, you who have not borne, for God is faithful and true. He who has promised will do what He says. Hallelujah! Praise the Lord!

CHAPTER 4

The Greatest Exchange

Imagine for a moment that you're in heaven. You're in the throne room, gazing at the Father seated on the throne, seeing Jesus at His right hand, enjoying the company of God, and singing His praises. You feel free. Every sin, every hint of guilt, every sense of heaviness has fallen off of you. These burdens have dropped like lead weights through the floor of heaven into the outer darkness, and you will never see them again. Sin is no longer an issue. Shame no longer has a hold on your heart. These problems aren't just patched over or covered up. You will never be judged, criticized, slandered, condemned again, by yourself or anyone else. All of those hindrances are gone.

In the midst of this great cloud of witnesses, your interactions are full of nothing but love and joy. There's no competitive spirit, no fighting back, no judgment or prejudices, no selfish assumptions, no need to defend yourself, talk about anyone negatively, or avoid anyone. Not only are you completely free from sin; so is your whole environment and everyone around you. It's beautiful and free.

That's an amazing picture, isn't it? It gets me excited just to think about it. This is where we go when we die. It's our eternal reality.

But what if you've already died? What if there was a way to already live in this environment as someone who has died to sin, to guilt and shame, to all the weight and heaviness of life in the flesh? In fact, this is exactly what Scripture says about us. We have been crucified with Christ. We are buried with Him in a baptism into death and raised up with Him in new life (Rom. 6:1-4)! We have already begun our life in heaven because our spirit is already alive there. Many of us may not be accessing or manifesting that life right now, but we can. We are so accustomed to thinking of heaven as something we experience when our flesh dies and our spirit goes to be with the Lord in heaven, but the gospel actually separates these two experiences and brings the second one forward. Even though our bodies are alive, we can die to the old self and live in the new. In reality, we are already resurrected with Jesus and seated in heavenly places.

I joke sometimes that we could call Romans the "Book of the Dead" because over and over again it talks about how we have died. You can see it all the way through. It's a fuller explanation of Paul's statement in Galatians 2:20 that he had been crucified with Christ, and it was no longer he who lived but Christ who lived in him. Romans talks about how we have died yet nevertheless live. We are dead to sin but alive to God in Christ (Rom. 6:11). Paul's use of words related to death is not an accident in this letter. He wants us to think about the ways we've already died to the old self and consider our old nature to have passed away so we can live in our new nature without hindrance.

Romans 6:11 is a great verse to memorize: "Likewise you also, reckon yourselves to be dead indeed to sin, but alive to God in Christ Jesus our Lord." The Bible is God's Word, a lamp to our feet and a light to our path, and it tells us everything we need to know to fulfill our purpose of glorifying Him and enjoying Him forever. This verse is one of those foundational truths for us in living the life God wants us to live. But it really takes some thought to understand what it means to reckon ourselves to be dead. This doesn't come naturally to us, and we have to retrain our minds to think this way. It's a continual process, and it touches on so many areas of what we once thought our lives were all about. It tells us we have already gone through that process of becoming citizens of heaven. We are already seated with Christ in heaven (Eph. 2:6). It tells us to go ahead and count on this being true so that we can live as someone in heaven lives—unhindered by guilt, shame, fear, anxiety, heaviness, discouragement, disappointment, regret, pain, trauma, bitterness, insecurity, and all of the other attitudes and emotions that weigh us down. It doesn't promise us freedom one day. It sets us free *now*.

Reckoning ourselves dead to sin is not a matter of making sure we don't sin today and then trying hard to live that out. Neither is it a theoretical or theological idea that helps us know that somehow, some way, somewhere in our spirit we are free from sin. No, it's a matter of actually allowing ourselves to enter into the reality and joy of knowing what it's like to be alive with God in heavenly places, even as we walk on earth. It enables us to live out the prayer of "on earth as it is in heaven."

So when we reckon ourselves dead to sin, we are acknowledging that we have entered into a new reality. We may have to remind ourselves often, especially at first, that we are no longer mere humans. We've been raised up as born-again believers, supernatural beings who have been set free from every fear and insecurity, every weight, every sin. Every time a lie comes around that contradicts this wonderful, glorious truth, we tear down that lie by reckoning ourselves "dead indeed" to sin. We might have to live among things that aren't in heaven while we remain in our physical bodies, but we never have to live as though we are stuck with those things as if they belong to us. Whatever isn't in heaven is no longer a part of our actual, eternal lives. Regrets, shame, dishonor, critical spirits, and condemning thoughts—we don't have to carry them around anymore. That's not who we are.

I quite enjoy reckoning myself dead to sin and alive to God in Christ. For some new believers, it sounds like a burden or a long process of painful self-denial. But when you understand what it really means, it's a delight. It's liberating. It's absolutely glorious.

This is a huge part of the divine exchange table. We bring our old lives and exchange them for new ones. We die to our old nature and receive the life of Jesus Himself in its place. We surrender the lordship of our life and receive Him as our Lord and King. That's the best exchange rate ever. And it's already done. Paul doesn't say we will die and be raised up. It's past tense. The weights have already fallen through the floor and are drifting away out there in the outer darkness somewhere, removed from us as far as the east is from the west. We can go ahead and live in the resurrection. Hallelujah!

Peace Instead of Fear

People in the Bible who actually lived this way acted as if they were already walking around in heaven, free from sin and all the fears and anxieties life on earth can create. They were not caught up in the mess and junk most people have to wade through. When I think about what it means to reckon myself dead to sin and alive to God, I fill my mind with the picture of their lives. We can be really encouraged and lifted up by their beautiful example.

Our foremost example, of course, is Jesus. He was fully God and fully man, tempted in every way like we are, yet without sin. He lived daily in a revelation of His true identity. He didn't spend His days worrying or in fear. When temptation came, He didn't own it or assume He had done something wrong by feeling the temptation. He saw sin and temptation as an external thing. He knew who He was and reckoned Himself free from sin.

We could spend forever looking at examples from His life, and thank God, we'll actually have a chance to do that as we stand amazed in His presence. But one example that comes to my mind often is in the gospel of John. It's right after He and the disciples had the Passover meal the night before His crucifixion. They are still at the table, and Judas has left to arrange his business in betraying Jesus. Jesus knows He's about to be arrested, beaten, stripped, whipped, spat upon, and murdered in a horrifyingly brutal fashion. Yet this is what He says: "A new commandment I give to you, that you love one another; as I have loved you, that you also love one another. By this all will know that you are My disciples, if you have love for one another" (John 13:34-35).

It's one thing to say those words when everything is going well. But when one of your close friends has just walked out to arrange your execution for 30 pieces of silver, and most of the others are going to run away from the conflict the next day, this is a pretty remarkable statement. He isn't pleading with them to stay with Him no matter what or emphasizing that regardless of how bad things look, He is going to make everything beautiful on the third day, so they just need to hang on a little while for His sake. He knows they are going to go through some confusing, disorienting, and truly difficult times. And so, in His wisdom, He chooses to tell them about love. He is actually describing the environment of heaven and urging them to demonstrate it on earth so people will know who He really is.

One of my other heroes in the Bible is Stephen. He was appointed as one of the first deacons, a helper, because there were some issues going on with food distribution to widows and other people in need, and the apostles didn't want to be spending their time on such things when they had other messages to preach and ministries to live out. So they chose seven men full of wisdom and the Holy Spirit to wait on tables, sort out the disputes, and distribute the food equitably.

That sounds like a background role, but the next two chapters in Acts (6–7) put Stephen at the forefront. He went about doing mighty miracles while making sure everyone in need got their portion. In fact, the miracles he was doing attracted attention from the Jewish authorities in the Sanhedrin at the time, and they thought he was becoming a bit too influential for the status quo. He was walking in a level of power that was threatening to them, so they stirred up some false witnesses to bring slanderous accusations against him. They argued that he spoke blasphemous words against the Temple and the Law, saying Jesus would destroy the holy place and change the holy customs handed down by Moses (Acts 6:13-14). But when they brought him in to the council and began to charge him with these things, they looked at him and "saw his face as the face of an angel" (Acts 6:15).

You can't wear a face that shines like an angel when people are hurling slanderous lies and judgments at you unless you're already living in the environment of heaven. Stephen had already reckoned himself dead to sin but alive to God in Christ. He was full of the Holy Spirit, who brings the atmosphere of heaven into our hearts and minds. From Stephen's perspective, he had already transitioned from earthly life in the flesh to heavenly life in the spirit.

So Stephen spent no time reacting defensively to accusations and trying to protect his wounded spirit and tainted reputation. He already knew who he was. Instead of reacting in the old nature, he went on to spell out the Scriptures to them and demonstrate that they were the ones who had unjustly murdered Jesus the Messiah. After showing them all of these things by summarizing the biblical story for them and pointing out the truth, "they were cut to the heart, and they gnashed at him with their teeth" (Acts 7:54). He apparently struck a nerve; they lashed out viciously. They were murderously angry at him.

But instead of getting angry back at them, Stephen responded as someone full of the Holy Spirit would respond who had reckoned himself dead to the old life and alive in the new. He gazed into heaven and saw the glory of God, with Jesus standing at the Father's right hand. Stephen's face was still shining like the face of an angel as he had an open vision of heaven. And as they shouted at him and stoned him to death, he prayed for their forgiveness.

That's what it looks like to be dead to sin and alive to God in Christ—absolutely free from the fear of man, not moved by blame and criticism and slander, not undone by extreme injustice and unfair treatments, and not even afraid for his own life. Instead, he gazed up and fixed his eyes on what was good, true, and beautiful. Even in that moment, he experienced the righteousness, peace, and joy in the Holy Spirit that fills the kingdom of God. That's a picture of how we can live every day when we reckon ourselves dead to the old and alive to the new, enjoying our life in heaven even now.

If we can just remember what we look like—if we can look in the mirror and see Jesus as our identity—and realize that we've been crucified with Him, not by our own effort or strength but by grace through faith, we will be living from another realm. We have been crucified, buried, and raised up with Him, and all we had to do for that wondrously new life was to humble ourselves and believe it. That is the greatest exchange ever.

I feel tempted to get upset when someone gives me a hard time on Facebook or leaves an insulting comment on YouTube. Stephen had people stopping their ears so they wouldn't hear what he was saying, running at him with violent threats and gnashing teeth, and hurling stones at him to kill him as quickly as possible, and still he was calling on God to receive his spirit and pleading for Him not to charge these people for their sins. I have been distracted and upset by just a nasty comment, but Stephen's face was glowing as he was being unjustly murdered. Who does that? Only a heavenly creature, a born-again believer who has been raised up from death into new life. He was no longer alive to sin but alive only to God in Christ, already living in his heavenly home, even while he was walking on earth in a physical body. He was a thoroughly new creation, and he knew it.

That's who you and I are too. It doesn't matter what you did yesterday, last week, or last year—or even the last few decades. If you will reckon yourself dead to sin because of the blood of Jesus Christ, you are alive with Him. He raises you up, gives you a new heart and a new character, and your face can glow with the glory of heaven because that's where you now live. Hallelujah!

My favorite apostle is another wonderful example of this kind of life. All the way through his gospel, John referred to himself as the disciple whom Jesus loved. He's the one who leaned on the breast of Jesus at the Last Supper. I just love reading his gospel and his letters because they ooze the beauty and wisdom of heaven. They are so full of the love of God. I could read them for dessert every night because they are so rich and full of delicious truth.

John didn't start out that way. He wasn't always full of the love of God. At one point, he wanted to call down fire from heaven to punish people. But he turned into an amazing man of God.

It's hard to pick out one example from the things John wrote because they are all so good, but one of my favorites is a section of his first letter:

Beloved, let us love one another, for love is of God; and everyone who loves is born of God and knows God. He who does not love does not know God, for God is love. In this the love of God was manifested toward us, that God has sent His only begotten Son into the world, that we might live through Him. In this is love, not that we loved God, but that He loved us and sent His Son to be the propitiation for our sins. Beloved, if God so loved us, we also ought to love one another.

No one has seen God at any time. If we love one another, God abides in us, and His love has been perfected in us. By this we know that we abide in Him, and He in us, because He has given us of His Spirit. And we have seen and testify that the Father has sent the Son as Savior of the world. Whoever confesses that Jesus is the Son of God, God abides in him, and he in God. And we have known and believed the love that God has for us. God is love, and he who abides in love abides in God, and God in him.

Love has been perfected among us in this: that we may have boldness in the day of judgment; because as He is, so are we in this world. There is no fear in love; but perfect love casts out fear, because fear involves torment. But he who fears has not been made perfect in love. We love Him because He first loved us (1 John 4:7-19).

This passage builds on that quote in John 14:34-35, when Jesus told His disciples to love one another as He had loved them, even as He was being betrayed in that moment. John is writing here about having the environment of heaven within ourselves as we live in our bodies of flesh. It's a picture of that weightless, glorious, love-filled scene in heaven's throne room, which we have already been raised up to experience. We can't love like that if we aren't reckoning ourselves dead to the old life, letting the weight of sin, shame, regret, fear, insecurity, and all of those heavy burdens fall away. That's why he says that the one who fears has not been made perfect in love. Fear doesn't fit in heaven. We experience the cleansing, liberating, renewing love of God, and then we can love others with that same love we've received. We bring heaven to earth.

The Mirror of Our Lives

There's a verse in James I talk about often in my sermons because it's so fundamental to living this new life: "If anyone is a hearer of the word and not a doer, he is like a man observing his natural face in a mirror; for he observes himself, goes away, and immediately forgets what kind of man he was" (James 1:23-24). The Word of God is the mirror, not our measure. It shows us who we are, not some standard we have to try to live up to. And when we look in the mirror of the Word, we see that we have been made like Jesus. That's the image God sees in us now. If we walk away and forget what we look like, we start living as though we are not dead to sin and still stuck in the old life. But if we actually gaze at the mirror, at the image of Jesus, we are transformed from glory to glory (2 Cor. 3:18).

Many of us have had a lot of experience in forgetting what we look like. I know what it's like to reject non-kingdom thoughts— the foreign currency of fear, shame, guilt, despair, and the like—and then slowly return to them as though I am still in the old life. I learned to put that behind me years ago, but I remember what it felt like. Those thoughts will keep returning if we aren't vigilant about reckoning ourselves dead to the old and alive to the new. When they remain there ticking in the background of our minds, they drain us of life. Some people who let that happen eventually give up on believing their true identity. They have given in to the enemy's lies. They have walked away from the mirror and forgotten who they truly are.

We need to recognize that we are like Jesus so we can respond to temptation the way He did, respond to the lies of the enemy as He did, and demolish false arguments and cast them down as He did. Jesus continually put whatever was good, true, lovely, pure, and of good report in His mind. When we gaze at the mirror of His life and His Word, we become what we are beholding. When our focus is on Him, we are transformed from glory to glory.

That's what it means to reckon ourselves dead to the old and alive to God in Christ. We remember the truth of who we are. We see Jesus and become like Him. As He is, John told us, so are we in this world (1 John 4:17). When we put our faith in Jesus, the Son of God who knew no sin but became sin so we could become the righteousness of God in Christ (2 Cor. 5:21), we become as He is— risen from death as the firstborn of the dead. He invited us into His death, burial, and resurrection, and now we get to live as He is without having to go through the punishment He went through.

Do you see what a life-transforming gift this is? We exchange *everything*—our entire former lives—to receive the resurrection, life, love, and glory of Jesus, which we can go ahead and experience *now* rather than waiting until our bodies die. Our spirits are already in heaven. We are free from all those heavy, enslaving weights of sin and all its distorted consequences. If we will reckon that to be so, living as though it is completely true in the here and now, we will love as Jesus loved, and our faces will shine with the glory of heaven. The world will know us not by our public criticisms and opinions and online bickering but by our love. It's a beautiful, wonderful exchange.

The Transformation of Love

In his first letter to the church at Thessalonica, Paul wrote about this transformation of love: "Concerning brotherly love you have no need that I should write to you, for you yourselves are taught by God to love one another; and indeed you do so toward all the brethren who are in all Macedonia. But we urge you, brethren, that you increase more and more" (1 Thess. 4:9-10). If we want to know what love looks like, we can simply look at 1 Corinthians 13 and see that it is patient and kind, it does not envy or puff us up with pride, it is not rude or self-serving, and it thinks no evil. Do you realize that if God is love and God is in us, we are love and this is a picture of what we are like? This love is not just a nice idea. It's how the world will recognize Jesus in us! It's a heavenly way of life right here on earth.

Paul says we should "increase more and more" in this love. We can't give what we aren't receiving. And the way we receive is to consider ourselves dead to the old and alive to new life in Christ. This is not a one-off transaction. It's ongoing, every day. We give love away and then bring our cup to God and ask Him to fill it up again. The more we receive, the more we can give. The more we give, the more we are able to receive. The more we understand who we really are in Christ, the more we are able to give people a taste of who He is for them.

I have to remember that when I'm tempted to engage in a conversation that's full of criticism and negative opinions—when someone says something ugly about my ministry or wants to argue about what God is doing in our network of churches—I have to stop and think about what it means to reckon myself dead to sin and walk in the kind of love that will help the world recognize Jesus. Am I conducting myself in a way that makes Him known? Are my comments going to be filled with new life and the love of heaven? When I do need to discuss an issue, am I dealing with it as privately as possible? Or am I venting unfiltered, old-life thoughts on a public platform? These become really important issues when we are walking in the new and leaving the old behind. We don't want to pick up any of those old burdens that have already been cast off. We don't want our online profiles to reflect something other than Jesus to people who don't yet know Him. We want people to recognize Jesus in us and know that we are His disciples because of our love for one another.

I believe a lot of Christians need to rethink the way they handle gossip, jump on bandwagons, and join in the negative talk. Paul continued his words to the Thessalonians with a reminder to lead a quiet life, mind their own business, and "walk properly toward those who are outside" (1 Thess. 4:11-12)—to stay in their lane, which means loving people with the love of God and treating them like He wants to treat them. If this doesn't work in everyday life, it's just theory. But we are never told that our new life is theory. It's real. We have been raised up in the great exchange to live as Jesus lives.

We are to walk properly toward those who are outside who don't yet know Jesus so they won't be hindered by seeing something that isn't His nature and character in us. That means that Christians who don't agree with each other should still overflow with love for each other because this is how people will know we are His disciples. Charles Finney once said that he needed to be good to the body of Christ because *it's the body of Christ!* I think we forget that sometimes.

As you can see, this exchange of our old life for the new life Jesus gives us is central to our testimony in this world. It not only empowers us to live without fear and shame, overflowing with righteousness, peace, and joy in the Holy Spirit. It also fills us up with the love of Christ for those inside and outside the church. The love that is shed abroad in our hearts by the Holy Spirit (Rom. 5:5) is shed even further and more broadly when we have reckoned ourselves dead to old things and alive to God in Christ. As with Stephen, our everyday interactions are free from the need to compete, prove, counter, and defend ourselves. We shine with the glory of heaven because we are completely free, full of love, and forever new.

CHAPTER 5

Encouraging Yourself
in the Lord

An elder in our church was diagnosed with end-stage bowel cancer. James was only 49, but he had a huge tumor in his bowel and secondary tumors in his lungs and lymph nodes. The doctors said there was no hope.

So we prayed, and nothing much seemed to happen. The primary tumor did shrink a little, and that was enough for the doctors to try an operation. They removed part of the bowel and inserted a bag, but unfortunately his bowel didn't start working again. Nine days later, he was in agony and terribly sick. The family called and asked if we could come to the hospital as the doctors were concerned for his life.

F.F. Bosworth used to say that faith begins where the will of God is known. We know from the Word of God that the will of

God is to heal. Satan comes to kill, steal, and destroy; Jesus came to give life in abundance. Everyone who came to Jesus for healing was healed. He didn't turn down any of those requests. So we know it is God's will to give life in abundance and to heal. That's where our faith stands.

We walked into the hospital room, and when I saw James I told him, "You look terrible; let's take a picture of this. This is going to preach really well. It's going to be a wonderful testimony." So we took a photograph, prayed and worshiped God together, thanked the Lord for healing, and then left.

The following night at midnight, Jesus walked into James' hospital room. James had a seven-hour encounter with God. Halfway through the encounter, James wondered why He hadn't mentioned the most pressing issue in his life. "Lord, You haven't mentioned the cancer."

"That's because it's irrelevant," the Lord told him. And James woke up at 7 a.m. completely healed. In fact, the surgeons had to do another operation to remove the bag they had inserted because James didn't need it anymore. That was five years ago, and today James is healthy and well and teaches at our prophetic school.

Nothing is impossible with God, even when you hear intimidating words from people who tell you that a situation is impossible. People have their predictions and expectations for what will happen, but God is higher than all of them. He is able to do anything.

That testimony of James' healing is one among many in a growing list of miracles that we have recorded to remember God's faithfulness. That's important to do because when you find yourself in an impossible situation, it can really strengthen your faith to recall those times when He showed up and did something amazing. Past miracles stir up anticipation for present and future miracles. They build faith.

Feeding on God's Faithfulness

Even when you have begun experiencing the double recompense God promises, you will still find yourself in challenging situations where you need some encouragement. Even when you have trained your mind to continually consider yourself dead to sin but alive to God in Christ, walking in the new instead of the old, you will need reminders of what He has done in the past—the miracles you've seen and experienced, the impossible situations He has overcome, and the testimonies of restoration you have already seen, and those you are still believing Him for. You will need to know how to encourage yourself in the Lord.

Most people are familiar with the story of David and Goliath. It's a familiar story of overcoming impossible odds by faith. The Philistine giant was threatening and mocking Israel's army every day, and the army seemed paralyzed with fear—until the young shepherd David came to the front lines with bread for his brothers. David was outraged over Goliath's taunts and realized this was not an affront to King Saul and Israel's army but to the armies of the living God. He refused to be intimidated and volunteered to go up against the giant and defeat him.

That much of the story is familiar enough, but I want to draw your attention to the moment when David was taken to the king, who informed him that he was too young and too small to win a battle against such an intimidating foe. "You are not able to go against this Philistine to fight with him; for you are a youth, and he a man of war from his youth," Saul told him (1 Sam. 17:33). In other words, Saul thought David wasn't qualified. And he was certain David didn't understand how impossible the situation was.

People, circumstances, the enemy of God, and even our own thoughts will come at us and accuse us of being foolish and believing ridiculous things. Like James and his family, we will be told that there is no hope, that we have no qualifications to pray in power or expect a miracle, or that our faith is nothing more than wishful thinking. But the Bible tells us that all things are possible with God, nothing is impossible, and again and again He has done something extraordinary. That's where those testimonies come in; we remember His extraordinary works. And that's exactly where David went in his response to Saul.

> "Your servant used to keep his father's sheep, and when a lion or a bear came and took a lamb out of the flock, I went out after it and struck it, and delivered the lamb from its mouth; and when it arose against me, I caught it by its beard, and struck and killed it. Your servant has killed both lion and bear; and this uncircumcised Philistine will be like one of them, seeing he has defied the armies of the living God." Moreover David said, "The Lord, who delivered me from the paw of the lion and from the paw of the bear, He will deliver me from the hand of this Philistine." And Saul said to David, "Go, and the Lord be with you!" (1 Samuel 17:34-37)

I believe God has called us to feed on His faithfulness like David did. Faced with a giant, David encouraged himself by remembering what the Lord had done. He understood that God's faithfulness in the past would translate into faithfulness in the present. He recognized the promises and purposes of God in the midst of a trying situation.

Later in his life, while David was in exile before he became king, his camp at Ziklag was attacked by Amalekites. The raiders carried off his and his men's wives, children, and possessions and burned everything that was left. Everyone wept, and David's own men, the faithful warriors who had been with him through the worst of times and remained loyal to him, wanted to kill him. And at that moment, we are told, "David strengthened himself in the Lord his God" (1 Sam. 30:6).

The Bible doesn't say what David did to strengthen himself, but whatever it was, it enabled him to get up, ask God for direction, pursue the raiders, and restore everything that was lost. However David "strengthened himself," I believe it must have included his memories of God's faithfulness in the past, his personal testimonies of God empowering him, which included his victory over Goliath and his frequent escapes from Saul in the years since. He and God had a history, and he knew God would come through again.

David would later write the words of Psalm 37:3: "Trust in the Lord, and do good; dwell in the land, and feed on His faithfulness." He was able to say such things because he had experienced God in battles with lions, bears, a Philistine giant, a raging king, and many other challenges. He kept track of these things because they fed his faith. They were the story of God's faithfulness in his life.

Developing Your "I Remember When" List

I was in Darwin in the Northern Territory of Australia not long ago, where we have planted a Glory City Church. The pastor there, David Ridley, was sharing a testimony of how he had been talking with his father, trying to recall some of the good things the Lord had done. He knew God had done some really remarkable things, but in the middle of that conversation with his father, he struggled to remember them off the top of his head. It's amazing how that happens; we often forget what God has done in our personal history, even though we know He has worked powerfully in it. So Dave decided to write an "I remember when" list—examples of remembering when "God did this" or "God came through in that situation."

I love that idea, and immediately some of my "remember whens" started to come to mind. I remember when I was 12 years old, right after I had found the Lord, and my stepfather had put a new deadlock on the door. I came home from school and got the key from underneath the rubbish bin, where Mum had hidden it. I tried to open the lock, and no matter what I did, no matter how many different ways I tried to jiggle it and turn it, I couldn't get the door open. I tried and tried until I was nearly in tears. At that point I cried out to God for help. Then, to my amazement, something turned just right and the lock opened. I walked in, fell on my knees, and thanked God for helping me. I knew God had opened the door for me.

To somebody else, that might not seem like a miracle at all. But after all these years, I haven't forgotten it. It has stuck in my mind as a memory of God showing up and helping me in a difficult, frightening time. That's the sort of thing we need to have in our memory bank. It isn't just for the big, amazing miracles that have happened, even though those are wonderful to think about and very encouraging. We also need to remember those tight spots that He got us out of, even if they were only important to us and no one else. They were personalized touches from God and very much worth remembering.

It's good to have an "I remember when" list on your phone or somewhere else that's handy to get to so you can stir up your faith when you need to. We aren't called to remember the sins, mistakes, regrets, and anything else we've repented for. Those are among the burdens we've given over at the divine exchange table and vowed not to pick up again. God doesn't recall those things, so we shouldn't either. But He does encourage us to make memorials and remember His faithfulness, and to feed on that faithfulness when we're facing a giant. We need those memories in our arsenal. They are powerful weapons against anything that would undermine our faith. "I remember when" lists can feed our faith and inspire us to remember that the God who did it then will also do it now.

I added a lot of "I remember whens" to my list over the years. There are so many wonderful things the Lord has done that I don't want to forget. I had recently been on Sid Roth's show, *It's Supernatural!,* promoting my first book, and Sid had announced to the whole world that, "this woman has an anointing like Kathryn

Kuhlman's." So whenever I went to a meeting, people would come from distant places on planes and trains to be healed, and we were seeing some amazing miracles. God opened deaf ears and blind eyes, raised up people who were crippled to walk, and it was glorious.

One of the places where we saw those kinds of miracles was at a three-day conference in Atlanta. A family came with a six-year-old autistic boy who had never spoken. I so wanted to see him healed, and even though his family had a wonderful time at the meetings, their son still wasn't speaking when the conference ended. They were very encouraged and happy about being there, but I was just so bothered that they were going home without a miracle for this boy.

My next meeting was a conference with Cindy Jacobs in Los Angeles, and she was giving a wonderful message, but I could hardly concentrate on it because I was thinking about this boy back in Atlanta. I really wrestled with God about this. I said, "Lord, I know people have asked You this for a very long time, and I know we're not supposed to get caught up in the 'why' of situations like this. But it's not too much to ask that You heal someone. Jesus healed everyone who came to Him. You said that we could do the same works Jesus did, and even greater works than those. This should be normal. This is not a big thing to ask for You; You can do the impossible. It's not too much to ask." And this conversation, a little bit of a wrestling match, had been going on for quite a while in my mind.

I was with some pastors from Glory City Atlanta, and as we were leaving the meeting, we were walking to the car in a dark parking lot late at night. As they were unlocking their car, a man walking two big dogs came straight up to me in the dark. Very abruptly, he said, "Pick a number between one and twenty-two." I was a little surprised; maybe people do this in America. But we didn't know each other, hadn't been introduced, and this seemed just a bit odd. I said, "Um, hello, I'm Katherine. What's your name?"

"I'm Michael. Pick a number between one and twenty-two."

"Okay, Michael," I said. And I picked a number.

He pulled out a Bible—I don't know where he got it from—and said, "I've got a verse for you." And he read the words, "and He healed them all."

I was so shocked, I turned around to my friends to try to explain what had happened. But when I turned back, the man was gone. I believe God was showing me that He wanted to answer that prayer even more than I wanted to have it answered. He wants us to press in and believe. We get caught up in the "why," the "when," and the "how" of things when actually He wants us to focus on the "who." He is the Healer, and we trust in Him. It was a huge reminder and a huge encouragement for me. It will always be on my "I remember when" list.

I wrote about one of my favorite "I remember when" stories in my book *Speak Life*. God was moving with so much power that many amazing miracles were happening at one meeting in Sydney. The Holy Spirit's power was tangibly present and the gift of faith was in the room. In desperation, one couple couldn't resist getting up and interrupting the meeting. They said, "Please, will you pray for our son in the hospital?"

I could see their desperation, so I started to pray. I immediately thought about a story in a book about John G. Lake. While he was in South Africa, he got a prayer request from a woman in Wales who was in an asylum. As he got down on his knees on the church platform, he asked the congregation to join him in prayer. He went into a very deep intercession, almost like a trance, and saw himself going across the nations to Wales, knocking on a door, and walking into the room to lay hands on this lady. Six weeks later, he got a letter saying that she had been healed at that very moment.

So as I started to pray for this couple at the meeting in Sydney, I thought of that story and began to intercede. I saw a vision of myself walking into a hospital room and laying hands on their son. I wasn't really aware of what was going on around me; I could tell I was in a deep place of intercession. And then when I finished, that was that. I didn't know what happened with this family after the meeting ended.

Seven years later, I was at a church on the central coast of Australia, and in between services a couple came up to me and asked if I remember them. "Oh, I'm sorry," I said. "I don't think I do."

"We're the couple that interrupted your meeting in Sydney several years ago."

"Oh, yes! I do remember that," I said.

"You prayed for our son who was in the hospital. We wanted to let you know he had end-stage lymphoma, and on that night, at that very moment, he was healed. He began to get better, and he's been free ever since."

Yay, Jesus! That makes me so happy.

I remember when I desperately wanted to see God do miracles and was crying out to Him for more. I heard a testimony of a young man who had prayed in a shopping center for a lady's deaf ear to open. I went back to my room and said, "Lord, I definitely want to see this happen." The next morning, I saw a deaf ear open for the first time when I prayed.

I remember when we took a team of 70 people into Hanoi, where you're not allowed to preach the gospel. One of my ministry colleagues had organized this trip and made a way for us to have government permission to hold three major rallies as "Christmas festivals." We saw 1,550 first-time decisions for Jesus! Our team saw the lame walk, the blind see, the deaf hear, and the mute speak. I had never seen so many miracles happen in such a short period of time. For the first time, I saw cripples whose leg muscles had wasted away getting up instantly after prayer and having their muscles regrow as they walked! They were being prayed for by team members who were hairdressers, housepainters, and all kinds of jobs that had nothing to do with professional, full-time ministry. They had simply listened to teaching on the will of God to heal and went out and prayed for people, and amazing miracles happened.

I remember when a woman came up to me after a meeting and said, "I've got a testimony for you." She told me about her husband who had come to one of my meetings three years earlier. He was HIV positive and had been prayed for by many different people and had not yet been healed. He was really struggling with the medications he was on, but I had a word of knowledge about blood conditions, and he felt the Holy Spirit touch him and the power of

God go through him like liquid, like oil running through his body. He was instantly healed and had the medical reports to prove it, and his wife wanted to share that testimony with me. Hallelujah!

I remember a woman in Atlanta coming up to me with her doctor's report and telling me, "Last year when you were here, you prayed for a heart condition." She had really bad heart problems that were going to require surgery. And she handed me the doctor's report and said, "Look, the doctor says I don't need an operation now. Everything is normal!" Nothing is impossible with God, is it? He is the faithful God of restoration, of double for all our trouble, of mercy and healing for all our sin and sicknesses. He has exchanged our old lives for the newness of His resurrected life. Hallelujah! Praise the Lord!

Stewarding Your Memories

What are your "I remember whens"? You don't have to come up with any amazing miracles or remarkable stories. But perhaps you do have a history with God or times in your life when you've seen His faithfulness. Have you ever experienced or witnessed a miracle or an answered prayer? Has the Lord ever spoken to you through a dream or a prophetic word? Do you remember times when you have felt the Holy Spirit speak to you personally through the word? Have you ever experienced God do something wonderful? The more you remember those moments, the more your faith is stirred up to believe His promises and see breakthrough and double recompense in your current situations.

Being deliberate about your memories and testimonies of God's goodness has a way of prophesying His past miracles into your present and future. As you recall what He has done in the past, not only is your faith stirred up, so are ideas about how to apply your faith to specific situations. Your memories of blessing take your attention off of the old foreign currencies that you've already exchanged and turn your focus to God's heart for you and His willingness to see that His promises are true. They motivate you to respond to the invitations He has put before you.

When you remember the ways God has walked with you in the past, you become much bolder in your claims for double recompense and restoration. You recognize the kindness of His heart, even in the "little" ways you've experienced Him. My memory of unlocking the door after crying out to Him when I was 12 has stuck in my mind all these years because it felt like such a personal moment. It relieved my fears and calmed my heart. It showed me His affection in a time of need. There have been times since then when He's met me at even more desperate moments when I needed Him more than ever. I remember when God has walked with me in the gardens and interrupted my tears. I remember when He has made me happy with His faithfulness to my children. I remember when He has spoken a word that unraveled all of my stress. These can be powerful moments, and they are meant to stick with us. We encourage ourselves in the Lord with them.

Before I had ever seen anyone healed, I was feeling so discouraged because I had prayed for two friends who had cancer and then died. I was ready to give up the whole idea of a healing ministry because I didn't want to keep getting disappointed. It was too risky. I figured I would just prophesy rather than get people's hopes up that He might heal them. But He met me there and reminded me that the Bible says we preach the gospel not with persuasive words of human wisdom but with demonstrations of the Holy Spirit's power (1 Cor. 2:4). That night as I was grieving and telling the Lord I was giving the whole thing up, God met me in worship and spoke very clearly. "Katherine, you must believe."

Soon after, I went to a women's meeting—one of my first preaching engagements—and a beautiful Baptist lady came up to me afterward and said, "I don't speak in tongues or fall down, but I have a tumor." Just the day before, a man who had come to our church prayed for me and prophesied that I would see tumors disappear. So I got excited! I had a word. I prayed for her, and the Holy Spirit powerfully touched her as she fell to the ground. She said that while she was on the floor, she felt a hand go into her belly four times. What I didn't know was that she had a six-inch tumor wrapped around her pancreas, and surgeons had decided it was inoperable. She also had cirrhosis of the liver. When I returned a few weeks later, I found out that this woman had gone back to the doctor, had a new series of tests done, and was declared free from any trace of cancer. There was no tumor. She even had a brand-new liver![1]

My point is that you can start remembering and celebrating God's faithfulness before you've even seen Him do a visible, tangible miracle. Remember, faith is the evidence of things *not yet seen.* Thank Him for the new life and the extravagant promises He has given you. Rejoice over the times in your life when you've needed His presence and He's been there. Celebrate the victories and even the problems and battles you didn't have to go through. Your "I remember when" list doesn't have to be filled with only major things, but God wants you to feed on His faithfulness, because if you steward what you have, He'll give you more.

This is one of the most important principles in the life of faith. When we steward what God has given us—the victories, the promises, the miracles large and small—He is faithful to increase them. He delights in doing exceedingly above all we can ask, hope, or imagine. He is our faithful Father, and He wants to be the hero of your life. He wants to encourage you constantly and bring to mind memories of the ways He has cared for you and blessed you. As you steward those memories of His faithfulness, He will take you into ever-increasing overflow. The exceedingly abundant goodness of your Father, always waiting for you at His divine exchange table, will manifest more and more in your life.

Note

1. This story is also mentioned in my book *Living in the Miraculous* (Charisma House, 2013).

CHAPTER 6

Partnering with God for His Promises

I found the Lord when I was 12, and it was wonderful. I was so grateful. But when I was 23, I went through a major spiritual transition. The Holy Spirit did a wonderful work in my life, and I began to have visions of speaking and seeing fireballs going out over crowds. I'd get on the floor to pray while my children were asleep, and I'd groan in the spirit as I saw multitudes getting saved and being delivered, people getting up out of wheelchairs and running, blind eyes being opened. I'd wake up in the morning with a vision of Hebrew words in front of me, and I'd have to go look them up to see what they meant. One was a female name meaning "wave." Throughout the day, I'd see people calling out to others who were lost and pointing them back to the heart of Jesus. I didn't know what to do with all that because, at the time, I was a housewife at home with young children. But it excited me.

"Oh God, if this is really You, talk to my husband," I prayed. At the time, I didn't really have a good picture of what women in ministry would look like. I was used to the pastor's wife speaking on Mother's Day and women leading other women in prayer groups. I needed some real confirmation because my vision for ministry felt pretty unusual. So I asked God to talk to my husband.

One day we were driving in the car, and Tom said, "You know, I reckon you'd make a great preacher."

Yes, thank You, Jesus, I thought. Then I wondered if God might also talk to my pastor, and I prayed that He would do that. I developed this scenario in my mind of being called out prophetically. Not much was happening along those lines in the church I was in, but a prophetic minister was coming from America, and because I was having all these visions I figured this was God's opportunity to put me forward as a minister. I expected the prophet to call me out and recognize what I was seeing in the spirit so the pastor could hear it and we could get this show on the road. It seemed like a sensible plan.

Leading up to that meeting with the prophet, I talked to the Lord about it a lot. I told Him how important it was for a woman to have some supernatural backing because this wasn't a usual situation. We're a special case, and we need a little extra confirmation to be accepted. I reminded God of how He led the Israelites with a pillar of fire, directed Gideon through dew on his fleece, and did signs and wonders to validate people's ministries. If this prophet called me out in some special or dramatic way, that would work really well. I thought that was fair to ask.

Finally the meeting came, and I was very excited to be there. I can't remember what the man preached because I was so focused on the ministry time afterward. When he got through preaching, he started calling people out. He gave some very specific words, and my anticipation kept building. But suddenly he was through with specific call-outs and opened up the altar for people to come forward.

That wasn't the plan. The pastor was supposed to hear the prophetic words given to me, and he wouldn't hear them if I wasn't singled out of the crowd. Frustrated, I went up anyway and stood in the line. The prophet went down the line prophesying to people one by one, still being very specific and saying some really accurate things to these people he didn't know. When he got to me, he said, "Trust God, sister." And then he moved to the next person, again getting specific and prophesying with a lot of details.

I was so disheartened. I went home and prayed, "Lord, this is important. Don't You care about the people who are going to get saved? Didn't You give me this call?" I just didn't understand why He wouldn't recognize my calling in public when I felt like it needed to be known.

I went back again the next night because the prophet was speaking again. I got really serious with God. "Lord, if You don't call me out tonight, I'm just going to put this whole thing out of my mind and assume it was my imagination. So if You really want me to go forward with this, You've got to come through." This was a critical moment, and I was very determined to hear something from Him.

Again, I have no idea what the prophet preached. I just prayed throughout the message. "Come on, Lord. I know You want this. Please come through tonight." After the message, the prophet started calling people out again from all over the auditorium. And once again, he didn't call me. So again, I went up to the altar when he called people up, still thinking this wasn't the plan, and I stood there and waited. The prophet came down the line, prophesying over this person and that person with amazing words of knowledge and detailed prophecies. *Ah, it's really flowing tonight,* I thought. *Come on, come on.* Then he got to me, paused, and said, "Trust God, sister." And moved on.

I burst into tears. I was so upset. My friends all felt sorry for me, and they got one of the prophet's helpers to come minister to me and have another go at it. But all this guy saw was a sobbing woman with runny mascara and a broken heart, and he just felt like the Lord was saying that my husband should take me on a holiday. And I sobbed even harder.

I went home and threw myself on the bed. I opened my Bible to a random page and said, "Speak to me, Lord"—not always a good approach, and I'm really glad I didn't open to Lamentations. Instead, I had opened up to the story of Simeon seeing the infant Jesus at the Temple:

> *This man was just and devout, waiting for the Consolation of Israel, and the Holy Spirit was upon him. And it had been revealed to him by the Holy Spirit that he would not see death before he had seen the Lord's Christ. So he came by the Spirit into the temple. And when the parents brought in the Child Jesus, to do for*

Him according to the custom of the law, he took Him up
in his arms and blessed God (Luke 2:25-28).

I was suddenly cut to the heart. I realized God had revealed to Simeon's heart that he would see the Messiah before he died. No one prophesied it to him. He just believed and was moved to go to the Temple at exactly the right time, where he saw the fulfillment of his promise. The promise spoken to his heart had been enough.

I felt so convicted—and a little embarrassed too, even in the privacy of my bedroom. "Lord, I am so sorry," I cried. "I haven't been willing to believe Your voice alone. I haven't trusted the Holy Spirit within me. I've sought confirmation from a man rather than resting in the conversation we've been having in my spirit." And I repented right there. I even told the Lord that if no one ever prophesied this calling over me, I would still choose to believe that I was called to go to the nations to preach the gospel, heal the sick, and deliver captives. I thanked Him and, even though it felt a little weird all alone, began speaking this out loud, declaring what I believed to be true.

Your Partnership with God

There are times when God does use human beings to counsel us and confirm something He has spoken to our hearts. That's a good thing, and it's wonderful when He does that. But we are not to depend only on that every time. I am so glad now that God didn't have me called out in those meetings because, if He had, I would have gone on to believe that's how it had to work every time He told me something. I would have made my ability to act on His will dependent on other people's obedience. I learned that there will be times when He says something in the depths of my spirit, and I can rely on His Word within me when that's all I have to go on. I love prophetic ministry and will always see it as extremely valuable. But God is looking for those who will trust the voice and promptings of the Holy Spirit for themselves. He wants us to take responsibility for recognizing the Holy Spirit within us.

It's easier to credit or blame other people for the things we do—to say we are following a certain direction because someone else said we should. But we need to understand that it's the Holy Spirit who has called us. He can use prophetic words to confirm and encourage, but He doesn't have to. If Scripture says we are called to preach the gospel and can lay hands on the sick and see them recover, that's a calling. If God puts something scriptural on our heart to do, that's a good sign you're being led to move in that direction. We cannot use other people's counsel as an excuse not to do something God is calling us to do. It's good to get counsel and ask for direction, but He is looking for those who will believe what He is saying to them.

After those two nights of meetings when the prophet told me simply to "trust God," I declared then that I would speak to multitudes in many nations, and thousands would be saved, healed, and delivered. Soon after that was when the Lord spoke to me about opening doors for me when I was 30. He told me I was going to see what He had called me to do.

Now that I had affirmed what God had spoken to my heart, I started getting many prophetic words everywhere. People would pull me out of a crowd and tell me I was called to preach the gospel to nations and heal the sick. And I would think, *Yes, I know! Hallelujah!* and thank them for their confirmation. I was told that my name would be in big letters all over America, and I thought, *Thank You, Lord!* God had already spoken to me that night in my bedroom. He had told me I would see the lost coming in and media would be open to me. I had His calling in my heart.

I remember seeing a television ad that God used to speak to me. A man was fly-fishing and pulling fish into his boat one by one. Then he put a large TV in his boat, turned it on, and a dragonfly came on the screen. Suddenly fish started jumping into the boat to catch the realistic dragonfly, and the boat quickly filled up. The Lord said, "I'm going to do a new thing, and you're going to see people coming *en masse* through the television. I thought, *I wonder who that word is for?* And the Holy Spirit whispered, "Stop giving away what I'm trying to give you."

These kinds of words and affirmations were God's promises for me, and I believe we partner with Him when we begin to open our mouths and declare what He has spoken. One of the proverbs says, "A man's stomach shall be satisfied from the fruit of his mouth; from the produce of his lips he shall be filled. Death and life are in the power of the tongue, and those who love it will eat its fruit" (Prov. 18:20-21). That makes our words very important, doesn't it? It makes me very careful about the things I'm declaring and decreeing when I speak.

I talk about this a lot in my book *Speak Life.* We've been created in the image of a God who created the world with His words. He calls things that are not as though they are (Rom. 4:17). So we are conforming to His image and partnering with His purposes when we do the same—when we speak words of life that shape the circumstances and relationships around us. When we declare the vision He has given us, we are affirming His purposes by faith. The Bible puts so much emphasis on what we say because if we can see something in the spirit, we can have it by faith, and speaking is an act of faith. When we have a vision and speak words that line up with what God is saying, things happen.

You may be very content with where you are in life right now. But the Holy Spirit in you is still dreaming bigger dreams. You have Christ in you, the hope of glory (Col. 1:27). That doesn't sound like a status-quo situation to me. He is dreaming of doing more and more so that the people around you will see Him and glorify His name.

Just to be clear, I'm not talking about doing more and more and becoming busier and busier. I'm talking about believing more and seeing more fruitfulness in your life—stepping into the "greater works" Jesus promised His followers they would be able to do (John 14:12). God has set a banqueting table for us and is ringing the dinner bell. This promise is for every one of us, but only those who believe Him and thank Him for it can receive it. The "greater works" are our destiny. We don't need to get busier doing more works; we need to see that our works become more like the works of Jesus.

A lot of people instantly object to this idea. Either they don't believe it's possible for them to see greater works or they come up with reasons why they shouldn't let themselves hope. They think it would take a really long time, they aren't spiritual enough yet, or they're disqualified because of things they've done. But we really need to get our theology straight on this and come back to the simplicity and purity of the gospel. There is nothing we can do to earn anything from God, is there? We don't merit our salvation; we don't deserve the extravagant rate He gives us at the divine exchange table; we don't earn double recompense for our troubles; and we can't work harder to get our prayers answered. All of that would be self-righteous, self-centered effort. We are told again and again by Scripture that there is nothing in the Christian life that we have to achieve in order to receive. So why would it be different with Jesus' promise that we could do the works that He does?

God delights to give His kingdom to little children. Children don't try to work their way up to the banqueting table. They don't sit back and defer to everyone else because they think they might not be good enough. They run to it. They squeal and shout and rejoice over what is being given to them. If we're going to have childlike faith in God's promises, that's what it has to look like. We read the Bible and think, *Wow, that's amazing! Do you see what's in here? I want that!*

God tells us life and death are in the power of the tongue. What are you going to do with that? He says the same works Jesus did, we can do also, and even greater works than these can we do. How are you going to respond? He says He will give us double blessing in place of our shame, pain, and disgrace. Are you going to think, *Hmm. Maybe, maybe not. We'll see?* That's not faith, is it?

Too many believers are still living in disappointments and rejections from the past and are disillusioned about promises like these. It's time to shake off the dust of that rejection. It's time to take those disappointments to the divine exchange table and receive the oil of joy and a garment of praise instead. It's time to shake your mane and roar like a lion because you're finally awake to the heart of God. He wants you to lay hold of what Jesus has laid hold of on our behalf. We don't have to work our way there. We simply need to say, "Thank You very much! I'll have that." And then pick up the mantle that He has given.

The Mantle of Jesus

A lot of people talk about so-and-so's mantle—the mantle of Kathryn Kuhlman or John G. Lake, or the double portion of Elijah's mantle that Elisha so persistently sought. It isn't wrong to think that way, but we don't have to believe for someone else's mantle. God Himself has given us a mantle. He tells us that someone other than Elijah was taken up before our eyes, and His name is Jesus. His offer to every person who believes is a double portion—the "greater works"—of what He carried on earth. We get to do what He did, only more.

Many people have longed for this invitation but assumed it was too hard. I believe an awakening is coming when people will recognize what is there for them. They will see clearly what the Word of God is saying and come to it with a childlike faith that says, "Lord, You are better than I deserve. Thank You for delivering me from myself. I'm going to pick up what You've promised and let You do through me the things You want to do for Your glory. Let's do those greater works!" It's such a good, beautiful, glorious promise. Don't just leave it sitting there.

That verse we looked at earlier about God giving life to the dead and calling things that do not exist as though they do is not just about God (Rom. 4:17). It applies to us. Instead of getting frustrated and wondering why things aren't happening—like I did when I kept wondering when the pastor was going to recognize my calling—we are being called back to a place of wonder. We are no longer to think like mere humans. God wants us to know Him, run into His arms, let Him fill us with His fullness and His overflowing love, and partner with Him to believe for the impossible and call things that are not as though they are.

The reason the righteous are as bold as lions is not just because we've accepted a theory or theology. It's because we've gazed into His eyes and heard what He is speaking over us. God never asks us to trust someone we don't know. He invites us to know Him, to spend time in His presence, grow deeper in our relationship, and enjoy intimacy with Him. Then when we read His Word and hear Him speak, we know the One who has spoken, and we know why His name is faithful and true.

That's why faith is not something we have to try hard to manufacture in ourselves. We don't work our way into believing. We just believe because we know who He is. We know nothing is impossible for Him because we have found that He is who He says He is. Faith is something we run into. We accept what He says and receive the faith He gives. Christ is in us, so the faith of Christ is in us, and that's more than enough.

Many people are disillusioned from the things they have misunderstood about how faith works. I believe God wants us to come back to a place of simplicity. He wants us to humble ourselves and begin to say, "Yes, Lord. I believe." That's what faith is, and it's rooted in knowing who He is. We partner with Him by receiving what He gives, believing and declaring what He says, and doing the works He has called us to do.

Being a Voice of Hope

David wrote a psalm of hope rooted in an intimate relationship with God:

> *Lord, my heart is not haughty,*
> *Nor my eyes lofty.*
> *Neither do I concern myself with great matters,*
> *Nor with things too profound for me.*
> *Surely I have calmed and quieted my soul,*
> *Like a weaned child with his mother;*
> *Like a weaned child is my soul within me.*
> *O Israel, hope in the Lord*
> *From this time forth and forever* (Psalm 131).

This is a great picture of those who are not distracted by the "why," "how," or "when" of what God is or isn't doing. It shows us what it means to tuck ourselves up into the arms of God, let His voice soothe, heal, nourish, restore, and fill us up again. When we're resting in the Lord like that, we hear His quiet and calm voice that fills us with hope and gives us a word of hope for His people and for the nations. We begin to rise up from that place of rest empowered to partner with Him in His glorious, miraculous work.

I believe God is wanting to raise up His people to be a voice of hope like never before. We have tolerated too many contradictions to His kingdom on earth for too long. A time is coming when the

God who is in us will roar and say, "No more!" No more power-lessness and faithlessness in the face of sickness, injustices, shame, and fear. No more of thinking the call and the promises of God are just too hard. No more of settling for less than the "exceedingly abundantly" God wants to do according to the power that works within us. We will begin to see His delight in us and speak His promises with greater faith than ever before.

We have plenty of encouragement in Scripture for this kind of uprising. Jesus told His disciples to have faith in God, and He gave them an astonishing promise to accompany that kind of faith:

> *Assuredly, I say to you, whoever says to this mountain, "Be removed and be cast into the sea," and does not doubt in his heart, but believes that those things he says will be done, he will have whatever he says. Therefore I say to you, whatever things you ask when you pray, believe that you receive them, and you will have them* (Mark 11:23-24).

I've seen this come to pass in my own life again and again. I can be rather pedantic about making sure my words are full of truth—people who know me would agree with that—because I believe I'll eat the fruit of what I say. I think God wants us to be vigilant about our speech and to declare things that agree with His promises and purposes. That's one of the ways His plans come about—people on earth agree in faith with them and speak them forth. And mountains will move.

We have to be careful to distinguish between weed words and seed words. What are we sowing into the kingdom with our speech? We don't want any weed words coming to fruition in our lives, do we? We only want to see seed words grow up and bear fruit.

That's why I'm so diligent to bring those weed words spoken about me to the exchange table as foreign currency. I do it regularly and often. Whenever something is spoken over me that looks like pain, shame, and disgrace—in other words, anything that doesn't look like heaven—I remind the Lord of His promise in Isaiah 61. "Lord, beauty instead of ashes. The oil of joy instead of mourning. A garment of praise instead of a spirit of heaviness. Double recompense for all my former shame, pain, and disgrace. So here it is." I am not reluctant at all to identify something as painful, distressing, hurtful, or slanderous. Even if it happened to be something I deserved, the promise would hold true. These are the kinds of things we often hold back from God by stuffing them down and not being honest about them. But He delights in giving us double blessing for them. He enjoys fulfilling His promises to us.

We have to recognize that these things have value at the divine exchange table. We think of them as our worst moments—embarrassing mistakes, painful slights and remarks, missed opportunities, heartbreaking disappointments, all things we wish never happened and place no value on. But they are extremely valuable in heaven. God receives them and pays us back with double blessing for the trouble they caused. This is foreign currency to turn in and receive back something extremely valuable you can actually use.

As we've seen, we receive this divine exchange by faith. But one of the ways we activate our faith is through our words—our declarations and decrees. When those upsetting things happen—instead of actually getting upset about them and trying to defend ourselves, arguing with the offender, compensating for the problem, accepting the rejection, or whatever our instinctual responses may be—we need to recognize the value in this foreign currency, bring it to the exchange table, believe God for double blessing, thank Him for it, and call what is not yet as though it already is. Sow that trouble in faith, and then go ahead and declare the fruit that is coming.

We can speak knowing that God is our Father and wants to lead us in His ways, letting our words line up with His will and trusting they will be pleasing to Him. We can pray, "Let the words of my mouth and the meditation of my heart be acceptable in Your sight, O Lord, my strength and my Redeemer" (Ps. 19:14). We set our minds on things above, where we are already seated in heavenly places, and rejoice in Him. Then we speak out everything that is true—not what we see with our eyes but what we know to be true according to His promises for restoration and the divine exchange.

I mentioned earlier that I've done this in many areas of my life, including the nasty comments people make about women in ministry, prophetic ministry, speaking in tongues, or whatever they like to complain about. Now I have great favor in the media and online. I'm on television all over the world. People get saved while I'm asleep because they hear the gospel in their own language, read one of my books, or watch a video. I have favor everywhere I go, especially in those places where I have been rejected and have sown that rejection by faith into God's promises for double recompense.

Everyone has experienced rejection. Everyone has been disappointed. Everyone has been embarrassed, made mistakes, heard insults, held on to regrets, felt insecure, been afraid, and suffered pain and loss. Don't let those things weigh you down like useless currency. Pick them up and bring them to the table. Remember what God promised through Zechariah: "Return to the stronghold, you prisoners of hope. Even today I declare that I will restore double to you" (Zech. 9:12). Hand that currency over. Receive blessings in return. Begin to declare them. Call things that are not as though they are. Thank God for double honor, double favor, double restoration. Let this become one of the ways you partner with Him—not only for His work *for* your life and *in* your life, but also His work *through* your life to accomplish His purposes in the world.

That is how God multiplies our blessing. He enables us to bless others with it. When we experience shame, pain, and disgrace, He gives us double recompense. But He also uses the restoration He has given us to minister restoration to others. Paul wrote about that once when the Corinthians needed comforting:

> *Blessed be the God and Father of our Lord Jesus Christ, the Father of mercies and God of all comfort, who comforts us in all our tribulation, that we may be able to comfort those who are in any trouble, with the comfort with which we ourselves are comforted by God* (2 Corinthians 1:3-4).

I am so grateful that God has healed me from the pain in my past and blessed me with double recompense for all my trouble. It is such an extravagant, beautiful gift. But now I get to give that same comfort to others and share what He has shown me about restoration. Not only does God heal our own minds, hearts, and lives; He shows us a way to let that healing flow into the lives of others for their comfort, encouragement, and faith.

So the double recompense multiplies, not only in your life but as it blesses the lives of the people around you. You can bring any shame, pain, or disgrace to God and exchange it for beauty, joy, and praise as part of your inheritance in Christ, fully confident that God's faithful promises will be fulfilled in your life and overflow into your world. You become His ambassador of comfort, encouragement, and restoration simply by receiving His goodness by faith.

If you will begin to believe that this is God's will for you, you will become a voice of hope in this world. You will have increasing influence for His glory. He is not calling you to live a small life. He is inviting you to believe that He makes all things work together for your good. Your faith pleases God, but lamenting the hard, difficult, and painful things and doing nothing with them is not faith. He wants you to put your faith in His character and receive double for your trouble.

CHAPTER 7

Waging War with Your Promises

God has always made promises. From the earliest pages of Scripture all the way through to the end, He has made promises for His people and kept them. When He first chose a man whose family would turn into a nation through which all of the nations of the earth would be blessed, He began with a promise. He told Abraham that he would become a great nation and have many descendants. Even when that looked impossible, God assured Abraham that his heir was not going to be a servant from his household but would come from his own body.

God also gave Abraham pictures of the promise—his descendants would be as numerous as the stars in the sky or the sand on the shore. He gave Abraham that vision to hold in his heart as a sign of the prophetic word. And Scripture says Abraham believed God, and it was reckoned to him as righteousness (Gen. 15:6). Salvation history was based on an amazing promise and a prophetic picture.

We're so blessed to have free access to this Word of God that is so full of promises for His people. In some countries, believers can be arrested for having a Bible. Most of us can read as many translations as we can get our hands on. This book is full of treasures, rich and nourishing food, invitations awaiting our response. We have been grafted into the people of God, and we have access to all His promises that have been written in Scripture and made available through His Son. All we need to do is believe and receive them.

Of course, if we don't respond in faith, the promises are just thoughts, encouraging words that might stir up our hope but never really apply to our lives. There's a difference between having access to the Word and actually coming to the banqueting table to eat what is laid before us. Knowing these promises is not enough. We have to apply them to receive the blessing.

The fulfillment of God's promises usually doesn't just fall into our laps, and many of them will be contested in our circumstances and even in our own hearts and minds. When we read that God gives double honor in the place of our shame, we need to posture ourselves in faith to receive that. When we see that it is Christ who lives in us, we don't really get to experience that unless we consider it to be true and act as if it is. When we read that "these signs will follow those who believe" and "they will lay hands on the sick, and they will recover" (Mark 16:17-18), it doesn't just suddenly happen unless we believe and begin speaking and acting on the promise. The first thing we need to do with a prophetic promise is believe, but that isn't the end of it. Very often, we will have to wage war with the promises we've been given.

Seeing, Speaking, and Receiving

When Gabriel visited Mary to tell her she was going to give birth to a Son named Jesus, she had questions, but she believed and spoke what she had been promised: "Let it be to me according to your word" (Luke 1:38). She was then able to conceive what the Holy Spirit wanted to do in her. When Gabriel appeared to Zacharias to tell him that John the Baptist would be born to him and his wife, Zacharias also had questions. But he questioned with skepticism, not faith, and had a hard time believing. Gabriel then declared him to be mute until after the promise was fulfilled. Why? Because words matter. Zacharias was prevented from speaking his doubts and unbelief and interfering with what God wanted to do.

We need to believe and receive what the Lord is saying. He wants His words to go deep down into our spirits and become solid, concrete faith. How does that happen? When we start to see a promise of God, we are to imagine it just as Abraham did when he looked at the stars in the sky and the sand on the shore. We need to envision what it's going to look like. We may not get all the details right, but we need to be able to see the weight and the scope of the promise and let our minds dwell on these things with hope and anticipation. It's important when we have promises to walk around in them in our sanctified imagination.

If, for example, the enemy has been attacking you with fear that your life is going to be cut short and you see God's promise for long life—"With long life I will satisfy him, and show him My salvation" (Ps. 91:16)—you can grab that promise and say, "Lord, here's what You say in Your Word," and start to imagine what it's going to be like when you're really old. Go ahead and come up with dreams and plans and envision the fulfillment of them. Picture what you're going to be doing, where you will be living, and how God is still bearing fruit in your life through your faith.

Take a moment to do that now. Envision prospering and having a healthy body and a sharp mind. If you're already sick, go ahead and imagine what it will be like when that sickness is gone. Picture specifically what double for your trouble might look like. Refuse to let the enemy sell you false pictures that contradict the promises of God. Just picture the promise of God. You don't have to know exactly how everything is going to work out and get all the details right in that vision. The important thing is to see it.

You have to begin to see it because whatever you can see in the spirit, you can have by faith. I encourage people I mentor to spend the last 15 minutes of the day before they go to sleep walking around on the inside of their dreams. God has given you a promise and a calling, so allow yourself to enjoy it mentally, emotionally, and spiritually. Before you go to sleep, set your mind in faith on what God is calling you to do and walk around in that vision. See it, imagine it, dwell on it, savor it, picture what it will look like. How are you going to respond when people are healed through your prayers and laying on of hands? How are you going to steward your gift of preaching or healing or delivering captives? How are you going to invest your time, energy, money, and spiritual gifts in the lives of people around you? What kind of fruit is going to come from the testimonies of your life? God wants you to see these things just as He wanted Abraham to see his descendants as numerous as the stars in the sky and the sand on the seashore.

Not only does God want us to see it, He also wants us to say it. He told Abraham to start calling things that were not, as though they already were—to start calling himself the father of many nations. That was essentially the command in his name change from Abram to Abraham ("father of many"). People who knew Abraham, including his wife, had to start calling him according to his promise. This promise was declared by everyone who spoke Abraham's name, according to God's instructions, long before it was ever fulfilled. Why? Because it is very powerful when we start to see a promise of God, believe it, and speak it out.

We looked briefly at a passage in Mark in the last chapter—the promise Jesus gave His disciples about speaking to a mountain in faith and seeing it move. The full story gives us a visual picture of that promise. Jesus had cursed a fig tree the day before, and when He and the disciples passed by again, Peter noticed that it had dried up. That set the context for Jesus' words about faith.

> *Whoever says to this mountain, "Be removed and be cast into the sea," and does not doubt in his heart, but believes that those things he says will be done, he will have whatever he says. Therefore I say to you, whatever things you ask when you pray, believe that you receive them, and you will have them* (Mark 11:23-24).

Jesus said to open your mouth and speak to the mountain without doubting. And if you look at the tenses of the original language in that last sentence, you'll see how envisioning a promise works. Whatever you ask (in the present), believe you have received them (already happened), and you will have them (future fulfillment). You mentally and emotionally put yourself in the time of the answer as you're asking, and then the answer will align with your faith.

So when you are looking at a promise, believe it is already done. You can go ahead and thank the Father for it. He said it, so you believe it. And you can wage war with that certainty and that conviction. You can go ahead and imagine what it will look like because, in the spirit, you have already received it. You can plan and behave as though it has already happened. Believe and decree in the name of Jesus so that you can receive in the name of Jesus. It's a done deal.

Pray the Promises of God

There is a fascinating story in Second Samuel about how to respond to a prophetic promise from God. The Lord gave David an awesome word through the prophet Nathan. It had multiple elements, but it ended with a promise to establish David's house, his kingdom, and his throne forever (2 Sam. 7:16). David's lineage would sit on an everlasting throne, fulfilling the ancient promise that the scepter would not depart from Judah (Gen. 49:10). David responded very humbly, gratefully, and worshipfully, of course, because this was an unprecedented promise from God and huge in the history of His people and this world. It would ultimately be fulfilled in Jesus, the descendant of David who reigns forever. Clearly this was something that was on God's heart to do.

But after David finished expressing his thankfulness for this extraordinary prophecy, he prayed that this promise would come about:

> *Now, O Lord God, the word which You have spoken concerning Your servant and concerning his house, establish it forever and do as You have said. So let Your name be magnified forever, saying, "The Lord of hosts is the God over Israel." And let the house of Your servant David be established before You. For You, O Lord of hosts, God of Israel, have revealed this to Your servant, saying, "I will build you a house." Therefore Your servant has found it in his heart to pray this prayer to You* (2 Samuel 7:25-27).

Why would David pray back to God the very thing God just said He was going to do? If this was God's plan, why did David feel the need to say, "Yes, do this, I pray that You will fulfill this word"? Because God wants us to respond to His promises with faith, to speak them out, and actually to wage war with them. He doesn't want us to assume the fulfillment will drop into our laps. He wants us to activate and go to battle with the promises He has given.

The way we wage war with His promises is to open our mouths and pray them. They become part of our prayer life, our declarations and decrees, our insistence in faith that His will be done. According to Scripture, there is nothing wrong with praying God's promises as though they are still in need of a response. Many of them are invitations, not inevitabilities. Jesus said to ask, and we will receive. He said to speak to the mountains in order for them to move. This may be subtle in Mary's response to Gabriel, but she essentially had the same response that David did: "Let it be to me according to your word" (Luke 1:38). We stand on what God has said by faith and pray that it will happen as He has said.

Here's what that looks like: "Father, I'm asking for this with thankfulness. I'm not going to worry about it and question whether it will happen. I'm going to ask. And I'm going to believe, speak, and persevere." We pray back to the Father what He has said to us and believe that He is true to His Word.

Many times we begin to worry, even over things God has very clearly spoken in His Word. And in our worry, we forget to actually ask. But God gives us such wonderful promises—everything we need pertaining to life and godliness (2 Pet. 1:3)—for us to use as a basis for asking. When we know His Word, we can know His will. And when we know His will, we can ask with holy confidence for what He has said.

I hear many Christians say they don't know if God wants to heal them or not. But the Bible tells us that the Son of God came to destroy the works of the evil one (1 John 3:8). It tells us that Jesus went about doing good and healing all who were oppressed of the enemy (Matt. 8:16; 12:15; 14:14; 15:30; Mark 6:56; Luke 4:40; 6:19; 9:11). So it is very clear that it is God's will to heal because Jesus is the exact image of God (Heb. 1:3), and He healed them all. Isaiah says that by Jesus' stripes, we are healed (Isa. 53:5). John prayed in the will of God when he asked that we would prosper and be in health just as our souls prosper (3 John 2). So we can take these promises and pray them. We can go ahead and ask God for healing and then thank Him for the healing because He said that's what He would do.

We need to have holy confidence in God's promises. I recently gave my husband a new barbecue grill for Christmas, and family and guests line up to get the wonderful things he cooks on it. Can you imagine someone coming up when he had cooked some beautiful food and only saying, "I guess I'll have some onions, if that's okay"? That's missing out on a lot, isn't it? God's promises are all cooked up for us, and asking Him for them is right in line with what the Father wants to do.

Ask and receive. Say it and believe. The harvest for God's promises is now, and it's time to ask, believe, speak, and receive. When the harvest is ripe, it's golden. When it's overripe, it's white, and it falls out into your hand. The harvest is white! He is waiting for His people to come boldly to the throne of grace to receive the things He wants to give.

Holy Confidence in the Lord

This holy confidence in asking and receiving is not presumption or arrogance. It comes from knowing who God is and carrying what the world needs from Him. Jesus was excited when He told the disciples it was better for Him to go away so that the Holy Spirit could come (John 16:7). His Spirit would then live inside of everyone who believes and empower them to do the works Jesus did, and even greater works than these. That's how good it's supposed to be for those who believe the promises and know how to wage war with them.

Jesus had holy confidence. When He was talking with the woman at the well, He told her that if she knew who He was, she would be asking Him for a drink of living water. That's not arrogance or presumption. He just knew who He was, and He knew He had something to give her that could change her life. In the same way, we need to realize who we are and what we have to give the world. We have Christ within us, the hope of glory. It's no longer we who live but Christ who is alive in us. We need to start believing that, not with head knowledge but with a heart passion, absolutely convinced that as He is, so are we in this world.

The Holy Spirit is bringing an awakening that causes the sons and daughters of God to wake up and realize the treasure and the glory we have within us, not from our own merits but from the extravagant gift of God. We need to be able to ask for God's promises to be fulfilled for us, in us, and through us, not as beggars who are thirsty for a drop of mercy but as children of God who are filled with His Spirit and co-heirs with Jesus. We need to know who we are.

Until we know what we look like, we can't have the confidence to receive God's promises as co-heirs with Jesus, or to manifest who He is in this world. Proverbs 23:7 says, "As [a man] thinks in his heart, so is he." If you think you're just a Christian who has attended a few events and heard about healing and prophetic ministries, you might be persuaded to give it a go and see how it works out for you. That's a great start. But it would be much more powerful if you reckoned yourself dead to sin and alive to God in Christ and realized that He is the one alive in you. The same Jesus who walked the earth and healed them all is the One who is at work within you to continue doing His works. You don't have just a little bit of Him. You have *Him*—His Spirit. He is your new identity.

That's why that passage in James that we've looked at is so foundational and important to our life in Jesus. I used to read James and feel condemned, and I had to learn that the Word is not a measure but a mirror. I don't read it to see how far I've missed the mark or even how close I've come. Now I read it to see who I am, which is who God has declared me to be.

> *If anyone is a hearer of the word and not a doer, he is like a man observing his natural face in a mirror; for he observes himself, goes away, and immediately forgets what kind of man he was. But he who looks into the perfect law of liberty and continues in it, and is not a forgetful hearer but a doer of the work, this one will be blessed in what he does* (James 1:23-25).

You can really condemn yourself with a verse like that if you're trying to measure up to it because you won't be able to do all the works you've read or heard in the Word all the time. You'll just burn yourself out trying harder and harder. But if you realize this is reminding you to remember what you look like—to look in the mirror, see Jesus, and go out and live, pray, minister, and speak in His identity—you'll find a strength coming from within that wasn't yours to begin with. When you know who you really are, you pray with confidence, speak with confidence, love with confidence, and do the works of Jesus with confidence. That's absolutely liberating.

Scripture tells us that Jesus is our true image. He's the exact representation of God (Heb. 1:3), we have been given His identity and His name (Gal. 2:20; John 14:13), and we are growing into His likeness (Rom. 8:29). That means we can have His mind

(1 Cor. 2:16), hear His voice (John 10:27), and do His works in the same power He carried (John 14:12). We can be as righteous as He is (2 Cor. 5:21); and, in fact, God already considers us to be so. He takes away every hint of our iniquity and crookedness (Ps. 103:12; Isa. 53:5; 1 John 1:9; Heb. 9:14; 1 Cor. 6:11). In the place of our sin, He gives us His own nature (2 Pet. 1:4). Any one of those truths—and there are many more verses to back them up than I've listed here—is, in itself, an invitation to walk out God's purposes and do His works supernaturally. Together, they are an overwhelming affirmation of who we are in Christ.

But here's the question: Is this how you see yourself? Do you look in the mirror and see a saint who is pure, holy, righteous, and beloved? Do you see someone who has been filled with power from on high to do the works of God? Do you realize that you're a treasure in an earthen vessel (2 Cor. 4:7)? Even beyond your mental understanding, is this how you feel about yourself? If not, you won't experience these truths as often and as fully as you could. But if you do—if you can learn to see in your spirit the things God says about you—you will never feel needy, rejected, or insufficient. You won't need to put on a false humility to let people know you're just a sinner doing his or her best. You will walk in holy confidence, overflowing with the love, kindness, and generosity of God. People will want to be around you to receive something of what you have.

When you have this kind of holy confidence, you realize God wants to give you even more than what you have already experienced. You recognize the promise of restoration and double recompense as just the beginning. You start to feel a sense of excitement over all the possibilities that are in front of you. You see the lives of Jesus and the apostles in the gospels and in the book of Acts as divine invitations to do the same works and experience the same power. You don't read the word and get discouraged because of all the things you're missing. Your heart doesn't sink because you can think of all the ways you shouldn't be qualified for these blessings. Your new definition of yourself is based not on your past but on Jesus, in whom all of God's promises are "yes and amen."

Your heart may still try to condemn you sometimes, but God is greater than your heart (1 John 3:20). In Christ, you can stand before the Father *as Christ*, with His name, identity, authority, and inheritance now attached to your new nature. You enter boldly into the throne room of grace (Heb. 4:16). Everyone who meets you is going to get a taste of Jesus in you because as He is, so are you in this world (1 John 4:17). You are confident not because you are proud and boastful but because you know who you are in Him.

Peter wrote something very similar to the words of James. After reminding us of all the exceedingly great and precious promises we've been given, including participation in the divine nature (2 Pet. 1:3-4), he describes the characteristics faith produces in our lives. Then he says, "He who lacks these things is shortsighted, even to blindness, and has forgotten that he was cleansed from his old sins" (2 Pet. 1:9). In other words, you've forgotten what you look like. You've taken your focus off the Jesus who is in you and begun living as the old self again. You aren't reckoning yourself dead to sin and alive to God. You're just reckoning that you're you. We need to remember who we are, live in the identity God has given us, and walk in the confidence of what He has promised and has already done in our lives.

The banqueting table has been laid out before you. Come and eat. You've been given great and precious promises for everything pertaining to life and godliness. You've been promised double for all your trouble in every area of life in which you've experienced it. You've been invited to the divine exchange table to turn in all the foreign currency that weighs you down and to receive all the blessings of the kingdom in its place. You've been encouraged to walk in the identity of Jesus, to do His works, pray and declare His will, and inherit everything He stands to inherit. You've been given promises for long life, godly children, health, abundance, and spiritual power. You are already seated in heavenly places, dead to sin but alive to God, living in all of heaven's glories while you still walk in your body on earth. If that doesn't give you confidence, what will?

The same spirit that raised Christ from the dead now lives in you. He has actually taken away your old life and exchanged it for His resurrected life. Walk in that awareness because the world is groaning and longing for a revelation of the sons and daughters of God. That's you—if you know who you really are.

The Happy Dance of Faith

When you know who you really are, you can believe God's promises and receive them as though you already have them. That's the heart of Isaiah 54—the command for the barren to start singing and celebrating the fruitfulness that is coming. He wants us to rejoice as though we have already received, because in the spirit, as Mark 11:24 says, we have.

That means that there is a strong connection between what we believe and how we respond. When we believe something, our faith should manifest in our attitude, words, and actions. We should actually get happy about what we don't have yet because we know we are going to have it. Faith counts on the fulfillment of a promise. So we can go ahead and take the singing, dancing, and celebrating we would have done when the answer comes and bring them into the present because we already believe the answer is a certainty. That's why God tells the barren ones to sing and shout, to enlarge their tents to accommodate the fruitfulness that is coming. There is great joy in the heart of one who actually, truly believes.

This command to "enlarge the place of your tent" is a call to go ahead and manifest faith (Isa. 54:2). The response of believing and receiving is not just an internal matter. It means getting started on preparing for the fulfillment. Not only do we "break forth into singing, and cry aloud," we begin enlarging our tents for the increase that is coming. When we stretch out the curtains, lengthen the cords, and strengthen the stakes of our tents, we are creating space to receive the promise. The barren—the unfruitful, the disappointed, those who are longing for something that seems much too long in coming—would never do such a thing unless they were counting on it coming to pass. They actually believe that "more are the children of the desolate than the children of the married woman" (Isa. 54:1). We are to sing and rejoice over the promise before we have it. We can go ahead and plan on the double blessing that is coming our way.

That's what David did when God told him the temple would have to be built by his son after David's lifetime. He went ahead with the preparations and set everything up for the fulfillment that was coming. Emotionally and mentally, he jumped ahead to the time of the answer.

That's also what my friends did when they couldn't find their passport. They looked everywhere they knew to look for it so they could come meet me at the border, but they couldn't find it. Then they asked the Lord to show them where it was and even rang up people to pray with them. But they still couldn't find it. Then they decided to dance, sing, rejoice, and celebrate receiving what they had asked for. They did a happy dance right there in their bedroom, and only then did they get an answer—in this case, in the form of a phone call from the wife's mother saying the Lord told her it was in a box under the bed. And that's exactly where they found it.

Can you imagine doing a happy dance over something you can't find? That's just a small picture of barren women singing and shouting for joy over the children they haven't had yet. There is power in praise. It aligns our hearts and minds with truth. It honors God by relying on His Word more than we rely on our circumstances and logic. This is how we fight our battles. Something happens when we start to sing and celebrate about what we haven't yet seen.

We saw that in the story of Jehoshaphat, who sent out the worshipers in front of the army when Jerusalem was surrounded by enemies. God had given him a word:

"Do not be afraid nor dismayed because of this great multitude, for the battle is not yours, but God's. Tomorrow go down against them. ...You will not need to fight in this battle. Position yourselves, stand still and see the salvation of the Lord, who is with you, O Judah and Jerusalem!" Do not fear or be dismayed; tomorrow go out against them, for the Lord is with you (2 Chronicles 20:15-17).

Jehoshaphat bowed down, the inhabitants of Jerusalem fell to the ground to worship, and the next day they went out to "fight" with their worship. The singers went first, celebrating the goodness and faithfulness of God, and the enemies defeated each other without Judah having to fight at all.

To paraphrase that astonishing story, King Jehoshaphat and the people of Judah did a happy dance in response to a promise from God, before they ever saw the promise answered. And breakthrough came. They waged war with their promises.

Amazing things happen when you do that, which tells us that filling our lives with praise, worship, thanksgiving, songs, dances, and all kinds of celebration is not only a vital part of who we are as citizens of heaven but a key to experiencing the fulfillment of God's promises in our lives. He is faithful, and He loves blessing those who respond to His faithfulness with holy confidence and joy.

Remember, we have been given the mantle of Jesus. When Elisha received the mantle of Elijah, he had followed Elijah persistently on the day Elijah was to be taken up into heaven, and when Elijah finally asked him what he wanted, Elisha asked for a double portion of the older prophet's mantle. Elijah told him, "If you see me when I am taken from you, it shall be so for you; but if not, it shall not be so" (2 Kings 2:10). Elisha did see him going up with the chariot of Israel and its horsemen. So he picked up Elijah's mantle, which Elijah had just used to part the waters of the Jordan to cross to this side of it, and struck the water of the Jordan with it again. The waters parted, and Elisha crossed back to the other side. He took God at his promise and did something with the mantle he had been given.

That's how we wage war with our promises. We believe them, thank God for them, trust that we will receive them, go ahead and celebrate the answer as though it has already come, enlarge our tents to receive it, and then do something to activate the promise when the time has come.

> That's how we wage war with our promises. We believe them, thank God for them, trust that we will receive them, go ahead and celebrate the answer as though it has already come, enlarge our tents to receive it, and then do something to activate the promise when the time has come.

A couple in our church had a baby who had a heart attack soon after she was born and was without a heartbeat for several minutes. The hospital staff revived her, but they told the parents that realistically it did not look like the child would survive. The family called me to come, and as I walked in the hospital staff were hoping I'd help them accept the fact that the baby was not going to live. Sure enough, this child was hooked up to all kinds of machines and looked as gray as death. So I told the father to take a picture because this was going to preach really well one day. We were going to get a great testimony out of this.

We prayed together, and then we activated our faith. We told the baby's mother to start expressing milk so she would be ready to breastfeed when the baby revived. When you believe a promise, you prepare to receive it. So for three days, this new mother prepared herself to feed her baby. And on the third day, the child woke up and was immediately able to start breastfeeding. Hallelujah!

My experience has been, again and again, that the Lord is faithful to do what He promised to do. But He doesn't want us to act as though we are helpless people just waiting for Him to do it. He wants us to be fully aware and fully awake, to rise up in faith and partner with Him in seeing His promises come to pass. He wants us to go to battle with them, to celebrate and rejoice and to enlarge our tents in preparation. We don't just wish it will happen; we count on it. We don't guard ourselves against disappointment; we plan for the fulfillment. We remind God of His promises and the prophetic words He has given throughout Scripture and through His people. We live in the environment of heaven even as we walk this earth.

Don't be passive about the Lord's will for your life. Don't just wait for double recompense to fall into your lap. Don't just hope the greater works of Jesus just start flowing through you one day. Don't pray as though you are shooting an arrow into the dark and hoping it hits the target. Recognize what is available to you through the wonderful, marvelous promises of God. Refuse the enemy's discouragement. Let go of the heaviness, the mourning, and the ashes of old regrets and missed opportunities. Don't get stuck in your adversary's strategies to weigh you down. As Jesus is, so are you in this world. That reality is available to you now. Your purpose is to do His works, receive His promises, and live in His fruitfulness and blessing.

Do you feel barren? Then sing and celebrate for the fullness that is coming. You are receiving full restoration—and then some more. Your purpose in life is to prosper and be in health as your soul prospers, to glorify God and enjoy Him forever, to experience all He has for you as a testimony to His faithfulness and His glory, to walk in the full fruit of His Spirit—His love, joy, peace, patience, kindness, and so much more—and demonstrate who He is in this world. All of that is your inheritance. If you aren't experiencing these things yet, wage war with those promises. Celebrate and live with the holy confidence of who you are and the blessings He is bringing to you in and through Jesus.

CHAPTER 8

Dreaming with God

I was spending some time alone with God a few years ago, thinking about the nation of Australia and its spiritual destiny. I was praying for God to send rain to this thirsty land and bring revival. A thought came to mind: *It would be so good if somebody would pull all the prophets together and we could begin to build relationships and hear from each other about what God is doing.* I got a picture in my mind of an underground sprinkler system that connected all the sprinklers that pop up and water the land. And as I continued to pray, I became more and more convinced that somebody should do this. I really wanted God to raise up someone to put this together because it seemed like a really good idea.

I heard the Lord's response to this idea: "Yes, someone should do that." And I realized that this was not just a wish or a hope; it was a divine invitation. It was a dream He was planting in my heart because He wanted to use me to be a part of bringing it together.

So I began to work on it, and God has blessed it and given it His favor. In our partnership with Him, He puts ideas in our hearts that He wants us to act on.

Receiving God's promise of double for our trouble is not just about getting back things we have lost and being blessed in the places of our pain. It's about taking that restoration and doing something even greater with it. He gives double recompense and restores years the locusts have eaten, but He does not stop just with a certain level of recompense and restoration. He is elevating us, catapulting us even further than we would have gone otherwise. He wants us to dream about what that means. This is restoration and then some.

If you want a great picture of that, compare the first chapters of Genesis with the last chapters of Revelation. Adam and Eve lost a lot when they disobeyed God and were cast out of the garden, and the human race has experienced untold loss and pain ever since. But the restoration Jesus brings does not just take us back to the garden. If you look at the end of the story, we get something much greater than Eden, don't we? We end up not just being in the image of God, but united with Him in an intimacy and joy that wasn't there at the beginning. God's promise for beauty instead of ashes, the oil of joy in place of mourning, and a garment of praise instead of a spirit of heaviness doesn't take us back to where we were; it advances us so much further.

So in that restoration, knowing how to wage war with God's promises and receive them, we don't stop just at receiving. We go on in the partnership. We take all the beauty, joy, and praise He has given us and leverage it to advance His kingdom on earth. We experience the righteousness, peace, and joy in the Holy Spirit for ourselves but also for the world that so desperately needs it. What He gives back to us continues to increase as we live in partnership with Him to bring His kingdom to earth.

So we don't float through life. We don't just wing it. We deliberately wage warfare in our spirits, minds, and hearts to bring God's promises to fulfillment in us, and much of that warfare involves aligning our minds with Christ. We have His mind already (1 Cor. 2:16)—that's one of the wonderful promises He gives us as we reckon ourselves dead to sin but alive to God in Christ—but to experience it, we have to recognize the lies in our lives and take every thought captive that exalts itself against the knowledge of Christ. As we align our thinking with His, He imparts His thoughts and ideas to us and we are able to dream with Him.

Living a God-Sized Life

When Paul wrote to the Colossians about the "mystery of God's will" that has now been revealed in Jesus, he included a very captivating phrase: "Christ in you, the hope of glory" (Col. 1:27). We know that Jesus is in us—we have been crucified with Him, and it is no longer we who live but He who lives in us (Gal. 2:20)—but also that He is not just passively within us. He is the hope of glory. He is taking us somewhere. So when we're in intimate communion with Him, our hearts merge with His. Our spirits become fertile ground where He plants the seeds of His dreams in us, and it is up to us to steward them—to cultivate and grow them to maturity. He wants our hearts to be in sync with His. This is where God-dreams are born.

Do you remember the mental exercise we did at the beginning of Chapter 4? We imagined being in the heavenly environment, in that beautiful place of blessing where all the heaviness, regrets, insecurities, fears, losses, and pain have dropped off and been removed from us as far as the east is from the west. In that place of resurrection, where we already live when we reckon ourselves dead to sin but alive to God in Christ, heaven and earth converge in us. We are spiritually in heaven while walking on earth. And in that place of convergence, God is bringing heaven to earth through the dreams He is putting in the hearts of His people.

For us to become aware of those dreams and recognize them for what they are, we need to wake up to the truth of our identity in Christ. He is at work in us to will and to work for His good pleasure (Phil. 2:13), and we learn to partner with Him there. We come to Him in worship and praise, yielding ourselves to Him in intimacy, and our hearts begin to beat with His. We open our eyes to what He wants to do, and that awareness becomes an invitation to partner with Him.

I believe too many Christians have for too long wanted to live a small life. But if Christ, the hope of glory, is in us, wouldn't He want to have a major influence through us? Doesn't He want us to change the atmosphere around us rather than conforming to it? Wouldn't He want us not only to enjoy all the double recompense and restoration He has given us and use it in restoring other lives, families, cities, and nations to His purposes for them? He has given us extraordinary blessings, including His own life and glory, yet so many believers have been hiding that light under a bushel, not realizing that we have the power of God within us.

That's why we can't just wing it. We weren't created to coast through life. We have to steward the presence of the Son of God within us. We wage war in our minds to refuse lies and align our thoughts with His thoughts. We take captive every thought that exalts itself against who He is, and specifically who He is *in us.* We receive every promise we have as His co-heirs, which includes not only His resurrected life here and now but also everything He won back for us—everything we get at the divine exchange table. We seek to bring our thoughts into alignment with His thoughts every moment of every day.

That begins as soon as we wake up in the morning and start thinking about the day. Worship is a wonderful way to start the day because it reminds us that we are already citizens of heaven and already recipients of the promises He has given us. Instead of starting out with whatever feeling we wake up with and then letting our minds wander through the day, we go ahead and set the tone and mentally step back into our true identity. Whatever doesn't line up with the mind of Christ in us, the hope of glory, needs to be cast down. Our thoughts need to reflect the fact that He is bringing heaven to earth for us, in us, and through us.

It takes some deliberate discipline to recognize when God speaks something to our hearts. We're so used to thinking of these things as just ideas that came to us. We don't give them the weight they deserve if we don't take time to distinguish the ones that might be His. He has so many wonderful thoughts and ideas for all of us, and they are different for each person because we are all called to manifest Jesus in different ways. We all express the heart of God with the same fruit of the Spirit, but His ideas for how we live out the life of Jesus in us are magnificently and gloriously unique to each one of us. We have to pay attention and not float through our days; we must pick up on the dreams He is putting in our hearts.

That begins with things as basic as our identity—our perception of ourselves. If any thought about ourselves doesn't line up with the truth of Jesus within us, we have to learn to reject it. Our mission on earth is to be like Him, to live as He lives in this world. Our calling is to manifest heaven on earth, so we have to recognize the thoughts that are heavenly and partner with Him to bring them to fruition here. We have such a wonderful and amazing Christ within us that we risk losing quite a lot if we dismiss His dreams, visions, and ideas out of a false sense of humility. He is glorious, and He wants His glory to show.

When God put into my heart the idea of gathering Australian prophets together in a prophetic council, that was an invitation. I didn't recognize it at first. I thought it was just an idea and hoped someone else would think of it and do something about it.

Something similar happened with my first book. I didn't expect someone else to do it, of course, but I did treat it as just an idea for a while. It had been in my heart as something I would like to do and hoped to do one day, and I even gave it a start, but I procrastinated for a long time. Prophetic people would come along and tell me I needed to finish it, and I would say, "Yes, I need to do that." But I didn't actually move forward with it. Cindy Jacobs told me I was anointed to write, and I felt motivated again to give it more attention. It took many promptings like that before I finally disciplined myself to treat it as a "now" invitation from God, and when I did, other doors suddenly began to open. God had been waiting for me to act on the dream He had put in my heart.

When God spoke to me about doing an album of songs I had written, I thought it sounded a little self-promoting. He dropped the idea into my heart, but I thought it might just be me. I felt like it would be wonderful to record some of the songs He was giving me, and I sensed His desire over that. But because it seemed like it might be self-serving, I told Him that the church really ought to call and tell me to do it. Then I would feel okay about it. I was afraid of what people would think if I initiated it myself. I was washing the dishes one day, and He said, "That's not going to wash with me when you get to heaven." I began to realize that putting it on my heart was His way of prompting me to do it. I was limiting a dream He had given me because of my own self-consciousness.

I know a lot of others who have similar reservations. They worry that people are going to think they are prideful if they give voice to their dreams. But has God really restored you with extravagant blessings and given you great and precious promises so you can have a private relationship with Him and limit His work of bringing heaven to earth in your life? I don't think so.

Don't be afraid to dream. God will humble you if you get proud; He has plenty of ways of nudging you back down a bit. But that's not the problem I see in most of His people. I see dreamers who are tentative and afraid of offending, even though their hearts beat with God's and are receiving His desires for their lives. We should never limit the Jesus within us out of fear of what people will think.

If we are going to steward His presence, we are going to have to learn to think bigger than we have normally thought. We will have to get used to His enormous and creative plans. When we pull down the lies that set themselves against the knowledge of Christ within us and set our hearts on the ideas the Holy Spirit is giving us, we will see doors open and be launched into wonderful and exciting new things.

I'm not advising you to go forward without sound counsel and confirmation. It's true that plans can fail for lack of godly wisdom. But I don't recommend waiting for people to hand you a microphone, come to you with a book deal ready to sign, invite you to speak at a conference before you've ever spoken in public, or whatever kinds of opportunities you might be waiting for. The world is not going to give you an embossed invitation. Probably no one is going to come begging you to step into your calling. If that's your expectation, you may be waiting a long time. If God has spoken, the ball is in your court. The next move is yours. You may have to wait on certain doors opening, but you still have to take the step to turn your dreams into actions. That's how God works through the ideas He plants within us.

I believe God is transforming the hearts of His people to give them the courage to respond boldly to His thoughts and ideas. When we bring our dreams and desires to Him, asking Him which ones He has put within us and praying for wisdom in how to move forward, He guides us into our next steps. We should always seek His direction, but we should pursue it with a "yes" in our heart, not a "wait" or a "maybe" that comes from our own fears and hesitations. He is raising up a people of "yes" who will steward the invitations He is giving us as we fellowship intimately with Him.

I've seen God do this again and again in my life and the lives of many other people. I've made declarations over some of the ideas and dreams He has given me. I saw Sid Roth's show, *It's Supernatural!*, and told my children I was going to be on the show one day. It took a while, but I've now received invitations and appeared on the show several times. I've seen doors open up to different media platforms and ministry opportunities that I had dreamed about years ago and said "yes" to in my spirit. I've learned to wage war with those dreams, including them among the promises God has given me when I've prayed and sought His will. I've recognized that those dreams are from Him. I've believed, declared, given thanks, enlarged my tents, and taken steps in those directions, and He is so faithful and wonderful to work them out. This is how He invites us to partner with Him.

Holy Spirit Dreaming

God wants to write His designs, purposes, promises, and ideas into our minds. He plants them in our spirits, and they come up through our thoughts and feelings that we cultivate in fellowship with Him. We can't just assume every thought and feeling is from Him; we have to recognize which ones are foreign currency and which ones are included in the kingdom of God—the righteousness, peace, and joy of the Holy Spirit. But one of the ways He imparts His visions and dreams to us is through the screen of our imagination.

That's what was happening when I used to envision preaching on a platform and seeing balls of fire going out over the audience and people getting saved and healed. Even though that didn't seem possible at the time, God was cultivating a dream in me. That was His invitation to believe, receive, declare, worship, prepare, and act, even though years would go by before I ever saw the dream come to pass. If the Holy Spirit had not revealed the truth of God's character during those years, I don't know if I would have been able to hold on to the vision. But I knew He was faithful and would fulfill His promises to me. Because I knew who He was, I therefore knew who I was called to be, and I knew the dream would come about.

The Holy Spirit cultivates these kinds of visions in our hearts and invites us to enter into them. While many people downplay these thoughts as "just our imagination," this is where God has invited us to see the things of His kingdom. We can see a lot of other things there too; not everything we envision is from Him, and the enemy loves to play out our fears, anxieties, disappointments, and regrets on those same screens. But when we are partnering with God, fellowshipping intimately with the Holy Spirit, basing our faith on the promises He has given us in His Word, our imaginations can be great assets. That's where God invites us to step into our inspired dreams, walk around in them, declare them, and believe them so we will eventually see them manifest before our eyes.

Learn to recognize divine invitations on the screen of your imagination. Don't assume everything is just you. Ask God to download His desires and purposes, and then trust that at least some of what is going on in your heart and mind is from Him. Yes, you will need to have some discernment there, but when you remain in conversation with God about it and search for your dreams in His Word, you can trust the Holy Spirit at work in you.

What does that look like? When you deliberately look at God and His Word and declare His purposes and plans, and when you are basing your faith on promises He has given you, you will find your heart leaning toward kingdom things. Let your mind wonder about them. Imagine what it will be like when people are experiencing Jesus in their lives and being healed at the sound of His name. Imagine how the gifts and skills He has given you are being put to kingdom use. Envision what it will be like for the people around you when God's love and joy are overflowing through your words and actions, and when you carry His peace into a room. Think about what it means to respond to people and circumstances as a new creation. These are kingdom thoughts, and they are very often the destiny that is shaping up on the screen of your mind through the inspiration of the Holy Spirit.

Be sure to root your dreams in your true identity. Identity always comes before destiny. Everything in your life needs to flow from you being in Christ and Him being in you as the hope of glory. It manifests as you reckon yourself dead to sin and alive to God in Christ. You look in the mirror of His Word and see Jesus. You conform to who He says you are.

Even though Gideon came long before Jesus, this is essentially the dynamic that God used to lead him into his destiny. Gideon was hiding out, fearful of raiding foreigners who kept stealing Israel's harvests. But the angel who visited Gideon called out his true identity—a mighty warrior—long before Gideon showed any warrior qualities (Judg. 6:12). Gideon had to know who he was before he could do what God had called him to do.

Jesus did the same with Peter, calling him a rock at a time when Peter was known for his volatility (Matt. 16:18). Peter would waver again, denying Jesus during the crucifixion, but he became a fearless preacher in the early church because his identity had been sealed and affirmed by the Son of God. Jesus called out who he was before he sent him out to fulfill his destiny.

What does that have to do with your dreaming with God? Everything. The things that play out on the screen of your mind can't be only about what you are called to do. They have to be rooted in who you are called to be—and, in fact, who you already are. Remember, you are dead to sin and alive to God in Christ. You can look in the mirror and see Jesus. You are righteous, holy, clean, pure, empowered, and called to do even greater works than Jesus did. If you don't see that in your own mind, cultivate that vision. Otherwise, you will not be able to carry the weight of your destiny. You need to walk around in the revelation of who you are so you will be able to walk out the promises and the calling God has given you. And you need to be aware that the calling could be much bigger than you thought.

Beyond Double Recompense

I earlier told the story of God's promise to open doors to full-time ministry when I was 30, and how the promise still wasn't fulfilled nine days before my 31st birthday. It had been a horrible year, and I really started thinking about that promise and talking to the Lord about how little time was left. I kept declaring it back to Him and waiting for Him to do something, and He led me to go to that conference where I met someone who wanted to mentor me and take me with her on her travels. The doors had opened just in time.

What would have happened if I had started to take action earlier? Might the doors have opened earlier? I can't know that, and perhaps God would have prompted me to recall and declare that promise with more urgency earlier if that had been His plan. But regardless of the timing, I began to understand my journey then. I realized that when God has put something on my heart, it's not a pie-in-the-sky dream. He is actually waiting for me to begin to take it back to Him, speak it out, worship as though it's already true, and take some steps in that direction.

I have found this to be true ever since that 31st birthday. I've put it into practice with church ministry, conferences, books, the Australian Prophetic Council, television programs, online ministry, and much more. It is God's will to expand our influence—yours, mine, and every believer's—because He wants His people to see Him as He is and create testimonies that show others who He is. He delights in bringing us into the dreams He has for us, imparting them to our hearts and minds, and walking with us to carry them out to fulfillment.

This is a wonderful way to live. It's so much better than living in heaviness, pain, discouragement, disappointment, fear, insecurity, and regret. This is the "exceedingly abundantly" that goes even beyond the extraordinary promise of double recompense. This not only restores everything that was lost to us; it builds on our losses and leverages them for ever-increasing gain. We get much more than double recompense. We get the life, the character and nature, the love and kindness, the faith and fruitfulness, and the ministry of Jesus within us. In other words, we carry within us the hope of glory.

Don't neglect the dreams God has given you. Don't dismiss them as passing ideas that would be nice but just aren't doable. Don't shrink back from them because they might make you look proud in the eyes of some. Don't assume that doors are going to open for them before you take the first steps. Go ahead and seek God's wisdom and godly counsel to discern if it's actually His dream. But when you know He is speaking, be bold. Believe confidently and courageously. Declare and decree with faith and assurance. Worship and dance and celebrate the fulfillment that is coming. Enlarge your tent and prepare for the increase. And take steps toward the promises, prophecies, and dreams He has planted in your heart because this is what brings glory to Him.

If you are going to steward the King of glory within you, you don't want to drift through your days, default to old ways of thinking and feeling, or just "wing it" moment by moment. You don't want to be careless about the things you say "yes" to and the times you say "no." You are being called by the Holy Spirit to draw close in fellowship and focus on what He is saying and doing. And you will be launched into a trajectory that's more exciting than you have ever seen.

God has more for you than you've ever understood. He is downloading His purposes into your heart. He's asking you to put some discipline around those dreams and desires so you can walk them out. He wants you to recognize what He's doing, speak it out, process it with Him, and take some action at the right time. When you hear His invitation, talk to Him about it. Ask Him to clarify and confirm. Pray for direction and open doors. And take whatever steps are already there for you to take. This is how you dream with God, and it's wonderfully fulfilling. The abundant life Jesus promised is better than anything you could have dreamed up on your own.

CHAPTER 9

Mouths Open Wide

I came across a verse recently that got me very excited. I've read it many times before, but I heard God speaking in a new way this time: "I am the Lord your God, who brought you out of the land of Egypt; open your mouth wide, and I will fill it" (Ps. 81:10). *The Passion Translation* puts it beautifully: "I am your only God, the living God. Wasn't I the one who broke the strongholds over you and raised you up out of bondage? Open your mouth with a mighty decree; I will fulfill it now, you'll see!"

We've been looking at God's promises throughout this book, especially those verses about giving us double for our trouble, replacing our ashes, mourning, and heaviness with beauty, joy, and praise, restoring the years that the locusts have eaten, providing extravagant blessings at the divine exchange table—even the exchange of Jesus' life in place of our own. And we've seen that agreeing with these promises mentally and waiting for them to be fulfilled is not enough—that we are called to believe them deeply, speak them out, celebrate them, prepare for their fulfillment, and take steps toward them. This verse in Psalm 81 captures this whole exchange wonderfully. God delivers us and restores us, and then we open our mouths in decrees and watch Him fulfill them. We get to see the words that we speak!

As with all of God's promises, this one is an extraordinary invitation awaiting our response. All of God's promises are "yes and amen" in Christ, but we are still required to give our RSVP— our "yes and amen" to what He has already said. When we have accepted that invitation to receive, we then have the power to speak it into being. We are not passive in this journey with the Lord at all. We partner with Him to walk by faith and declare those things that are not as though they are. That is how He created the world, and He has made us in His image to be creative with our words too.

Jesus said He only did what He saw the Father doing and only spoke what He heard the Father saying (John 5:19; 12:49-50). So when we hear the Father saying something—when we read a promise in His Word or receive prophetic promises and declarations that line up with His Word—we are invited to speak it out. He wants us not to behave as passive believers or, even worse, as victims of circumstances. He wants us to walk in power and authority and recognize the effectiveness of our words.

As a prophetic person, I know the power prophetic words can have and how they activate something in the spiritual realm. But I also understand that words have power even when we're not intending to prophesy. When we are complaining about a situation, describing how bad things are, talking negatively about someone else, and all of that "small talk" that might not be very uplifting if we aren't in a good mood, something is happening. Our words are accomplishing things, and not in the way we want. We need to be very careful about what we say because our words have creative power in our lives, relationships, and circumstances.

Scripture tells us that God made the world with His words. As those who are made in His image—and have been restored to the image of God in Christ, who is the perfect picture of the Father (Heb. 1:3)—we have been given creative power in our words. God is waiting for us to wake up to the fact that we are fully able to participate in the divine nature (2 Pet. 1:4). We've been set free from sin and are alive to God in Christ, and we have every reason to behave as people who are not just surviving in this world but are ruling and reigning with Him. As His ambassadors, we can open our mouths, speak His purposes into the earth, and create with the power of words.

I teach this often at our church in Brisbane and wherever I travel around the world, and it is so encouraging to hear stories from people who have been coming into agreement with God's Word and seeing things happen as a result. As believers are becoming aware of the way they use their words—and how they have perhaps carelessly misused them in the past—they are finding that circumstances shift under the power and authority of God through the words of His people. We have a new nature, and we can live and speak from that nature as those who are restored, doubly blessed, and provided with abundant promises of provision, protection, life, and influence. More and more believers are walking in the holy confidence God has invited them to enjoy.

The Truth About You

I like to play a game with family and friends. We go around a circle and make decrees. We call things that are not as though they are and declare the things God has put on our hearts to see. We express His promises out loud and add our "yes and amen" to what He has already given us in and through Jesus. It's a wonderfully encouraging game that actually accomplishes quite a lot in our lives, the lives of others, and in the world.

Speaking the Word of the Lord is not just a vain exercise. It's not something we do just hoping some of what we say will come to pass. It isn't a magic trick or talking ourselves into something through positive thinking. We aren't trying to convince ourselves of something that isn't true; we're reminding ourselves of what is true—or what can and should be true if heaven is manifesting on earth. We actually speak out in faith the promises and prophecies God has given us, believing that these things are the will of God and that we can have whatever we have asked according to His will. If faith begins where the will of God is known, we have a lot to go on because He has expressed much of His will very clearly. That's why God has made His will known to prophets (Amos 3:7) and why He tells us to pray—so human beings will speak out what He wants to do. Putting a human voice to a divine reality, our words activate His will in the spiritual and physical realm.

With that in mind, I want to do something a little different in this chapter. The following pages are less about teaching principles than they are about providing examples. It's time to apply some of what we've been discussing. I want to go through some decrees in this chapter that will help you get started and activate this ministry of speaking into your life to begin to see double recompense—not just so you can know about God's restoration and all the dreams and promises that go beyond it, but so you can begin experiencing them right now.

If you can learn to live with a mouth full of the Lord's words, speaking creatively and powerfully into all of your circumstances and relationships, I think you will be surprised at how radically situations shift. You will pray with greater power when you declare and decree in faith what God has promised, and you will also discover the positive influence your words can have on the world around you.

Here are a few of the promises you can begin to decree as the redeemed of the Lord. As part of our salvation, we are given a full array of remarkable, astonishing promises in Christ. We have already looked at many of them, but no matter how familiar these are, they are worth remembering, claiming, and speaking over ourselves. They will help you let go of the foreign currency you've already brought to the exchange table by undoing shame, pain, disgrace, regret, and fear—those things you have given to God and have promised not to pick up again. These present-day spiritual realities will help get you started with declaring truth over yourself daily:

I have a new heart (Ezek. 36:26).

Did you know your heart is pure? According to Ezekiel, it is. Jeremiah said the heart was desperately wicked, but he was talking about our old nature. In the new covenant, which Jeremiah also wrote about, God puts His law in our hearts (Jer. 31:33). It's possible for a believer to live from the old heart, but when we reckon ourselves dead to sin and alive to Christ, we can live from our new nature. Our sin has been covered, and we now have a new nature and the mind of Christ. It is no longer we who live but He who lives within, moving and working for His good pleasure. Christ the hope of glory is in us.

I'm a partaker of the divine nature (2 Pet. 1:3).

Remember, God has given you great and precious promises for everything pertaining to life and godliness. "Everything" covers a lot, doesn't it? Nothing is left out. But these promises don't do us much good if we don't remember what we look like—it is like looking in the mirror and then walking away and forgetting who we really are. We continually gaze into the Word and into the face of Jesus to see who we are (identity) so that we can walk it out (calling).

It is no longer I who live but Christ who lives in me (Gal. 2:20).

Reminding yourself of what you look like prepares you to walk in the nature and holiness of Christ, doing His works and speaking His words. It is powerful to speak to your soul about your true identity, reminding yourself that it is Christ, the hope of glory, who lives in you. When you really believe this, you can see many of your motives and ideas as His, not your own, and begin to trust them. You will learn to dream with Him.

I am free from sin (Rom. 6:7, 18, 22).

This doesn't mean you haven't done anything wrong and won't do something wrong again in the future, but God sees you as completely free. If you've done something wrong, talk to Him about it. Thank Him that He has already paid for it. Refuse to believe the lie that now you must measure up to God's standards or become requalified to do His works. Do not let guilt and shame back in. On your behalf, Jesus has already done all the measuring up that will ever need to be done. Now you can just thank Him for being made righteous, pure, and holy.

I am holy, blameless, and above reproach before Him (Col. 1:22).

This is not dependent on how you feel. It's true because it's what God says about you. Jesus' blood was spilled to count you righteous before God. Don't let your feelings minimize that amazing blessing. Constantly remind your soul that you are clean and pure.

According to the new covenant, God has not just covered our sin. He has taken it away. He has removed it as far as the east is from the west (Ps. 103:12). Jesus "was wounded for our transgressions, He was bruised for our iniquities" (Isa. 53:5). "Transgressions" refers to our sins; "iniquities" means our "crookedness." Jesus was crushed so our old nature would be destroyed and we could become new in Him. That means you have a clean and pure heart.

If you don't believe that, you are laboring under a lie. It will cause you to distance yourself from God and believe lies about Him—that He is just tolerating you, for example, because He has to. But the blood of Jesus was spilled to change us from the inside out so we could become the righteousness of God in Christ (2 Cor. 5:21). So even if our own heart condemns us, He is greater than our heart (1 John 3:20). That may be hard to believe for people who are used to walking in condemnation, but it's true. It's what the Word of God says.

I have become the righteousness of God in Christ (2 Cor. 5:21).

Thank Him that you have not only been forgiven; you have also become the righteousness of God. The whole verse says, "He made Him who knew no sin to be sin for us, that we might become the righteousness of God in Him." That's really an astonishing gift. Sin has been removed from you as far as the east is from the west. You are not defined by sin anymore. You are defined by Jesus and walk by faith in Him.

As He is, so am I in this world (1 John 4:17).

Because of all the statements above, you can walk in the works that Jesus did. You reckon yourself dead to sin—count it as absolutely true, no matter what evidence you think you see in your own thoughts and actions—and alive to God in Christ. His Spirit is in you, working for His good pleasure. By faith, you now become a manifestation of Jesus in this world.

We are not hoping for or trying to become these things. They are present-day realities because we have given our lives to Jesus and exchanged our own lives for His. All of our weakness, sin, shame, guilt, burdens, regrets, heaviness, bitterness, and disappointments have been handed over to Him at the divine exchange table, and in return we've receive His life. He is now our identity. We grow into His image by gazing at Him (2 Cor. 3:18) and remembering who we really are (James 1: 23-24; 2 Pet. 1:9).

I spent quite a bit of time going through Romans a few years ago, looking at it in several translations and chewing every word, deliberately slowing myself down to let it sink in. It became so abundantly clear that in the crucifixion and resurrection of Jesus, we died, were buried, and were raised up together with Him as new creations. We are now the just who walk by faith. We are never again trying to earn our righteousness. We are saved by grace through faith, already and forever. The word *salvation* in Romans is comprehensive—our transgressions, iniquities, everything! Jesus accomplished our spiritual salvation, our healing, our deliverance, and anything we needed saving from, and He is our peace. Hallelujah!

God's Will for You

I love to pray the Bible. You can read and come across verses that are encouraging thoughts and what you needed to hear that day. That can be very helpful. But why not take it further? Speak it out. It's your primary source for declarations and decrees. Pray into it throughout the day and night in the weeks ahead. These are weapons that are mighty to the pulling down of strongholds (2 Cor. 10:4-5). They demolish the lies of the enemy that are trying to ensnare you in discouraging, futile ways of thinking. We need to wage war not only with God's promises but with every truth He gives us.

Temptation comes in many different forms—internal thoughts and perceptions, external enticements, attitudes and opinions from the world around us—but none of them, even the ones we think are internal, are part of our new nature. They are foreign to us, not at all who we are. We have the power to answer temptation like Jesus did—with the Word of the Lord. We can speak the Word and see lies dispelled. We don't just ignore the lies, and we don't just think, *Oh, what a terrible thought.* We cast them down by speaking the truth.

When temptation comes, many Christians feel bad that they have been tempted. They associate the temptation itself with guilt. But Jesus was tempted like we are, and He wasn't guilty. He simply cast down the argument with the Word of the Lord. We cannot afford to take on the guilt that the enemy wants to bring into our lives through temptation. Temptation is external, even though he will try to convince you that it is part of who you are. It is a lie, and we can tell our feelings to line up with the truth of God. We can remind him that we are the redeemed of the Lord according to the Word of God.

Remember, the kingdom of God is righteousness, peace, and joy in the Holy Spirit. Everything that doesn't fit that description needs to be cast down. God has given us weapons that overcome and destroy the works of the devil. No weapon raised against you will prosper (Isa. 54:17). God has given us the tools to destroy every one of them and render them futile. We are not to be passive readers of the Word. We are to get up and fight with it.

That's why it is so important not to make decrees and prophesy things that are simply what we see. It does no good to talk about how bad things are. We are made in the image of God, who gives life to the dead and calls things that do not yet exist as though they do (Rom. 4:17). We cannot afford to miss the opportunity to create with our words. We have to learn to be very deliberate about this, even in our casual conversations. Over time, we receive the things we speak.

Just as we looked at some of God's statements about our identity and righteousness that we can decree over ourselves, we can also discover many statements about His will and purposes for us and decree them. If we are going to receive the things we speak, we need to be intentional to shape our lives with our words. You'll discover many wonderful truths in God's Word to declare over your calling, your relationships, and your circumstances. Here are a few to get started:

My ways please the Lord, and God has made even my enemies to live at peace with me (Prov. 16:7).

My soul needs to be reminded of this reality. I am not the victim of random events or people's animosities. I understand that Jesus had enemies who were clearly not at peace with Him, even though His ways very much pleased the Lord. But His enemies never got the upper hand on Him until His divine appointment with the cross, and God can shelter us from adversaries too. Just as Jesus walked through a hostile crowd at Nazareth and escaped (Luke 4:28-30), we can rest in God's protective care. When we walk in ways that please the Lord, we can trust Him with everything else in our lives and overcome any strife that is aimed against us.

Everyone I lay hands on is healed in Jesus' name (Matt. 8:16; 12:15; 14:14; 15:30; Mark 6:56; Luke 4:40; 6:19; 9:11).

Scripture tells us that everyone who came to Jesus received healing. Because this is true of Jesus, and as you and I are as He is in this world, we can personalize this and decree it for ourselves as well. I've written down some of the verses that say, "He healed them all" (or something similar) and read them often. I daily declare that it is no longer I who live but He who lives in me. So I pray with the expectation that everyone I pray for will be healed.

I am deeply loved and experience God's love for me in ever-increasing ways (1 John 3:1; 4:10; Eph. 2:4-5).

When the enemy is lying to you and saying no one loves you, you're all alone, no one understands, everything is going wrong, and all those discouraging thoughts he puts into our minds, just remind him of how incredibly loved you are by the Father—so much that He gave the life of His Son for you. He has promised you a hope and a future (Jer. 29:11), and nothing the enemy says or does can change that. You are beloved and accepted, blessed with every spiritual blessing and seated in heavenly places with Christ (Eph. 1:3-6; 2:6). No lies can undo what the Father has done for you because of His magnificent love for you.

I'm surrounded by the favor of the Lord as with a shield (Ps. 5:12).

This is one of my favorites. I love to walk around with this promise on the screen of my mind and envision God's protection over me. No weapon formed against His people will prosper (Isa. 54:17). God doesn't guarantee that we will never have weapons raised against us or face hardship. In fact, Psalm 34:19 says, "Many are the afflictions of the righteous, but the Lord delivers him out of them all." He promises that He will protect us and deliver us. These are powerful declarations to make.

I have the mind of Christ (1 Cor. 2:16).

Because the mind of Jesus is in me, I can instinctively believe the best about people and have pure thoughts and motives. If God is love, then I can be love too—patient, kind, long-suffering, not self-serving, always rejoicing in the truth and believing good things (1 Cor. 13:4-7). When people encounter me, they can experience the love, joy, and peace of Christ within me because I'm speaking it, creating it, and making room for it. I'm following in the footsteps of the Lord and letting Him live His life in me.

Can you see how declaring and decreeing these things is different from just hoping they will happen? We need to step into them. Others, like laying our hands on people and seeing them healed, are promises and possibilities for us, invitations we can experience by faith. When we say what we know to be true, we are attaching our faith to it and letting our words create what we have seen in the Spirit according to the will and Word of God. We can know these things are coming to pass.

The Word of the Lord is a lamp to our feet and a light to our path (Ps. 119:105), and speaking it out in faith is like turning on the light. I declare that all my family members are saved and walking in freedom and joy. I declare that He who has purposed it will also do it (Isa. 46:11). When we know this is His will, we can pray for people with confidence that God is responding to our faith and doing something in their lives. He is restoring lives in answer to our prayers and decrees. This is really too good of an opportunity to waste and an amazing privilege to partner with Him in our words.

The Desires of Your Heart

While many Christians believe He is only interested in taking care of our needs and giving us basic levels of protection and provision, His own Word is so much more generous than that. You can declare that:

God gives me the desires of my heart (Ps. 37:4).

We don't pray as orphans or beggars, hoping God will give us just what we need to get by. We are adopted as children, and He is very generous with us as our adoring Father who loves to bless us. One of His promises is to give us the desires of our hearts, and because we can create with His words, we can speak out our desires as we do with His promises. When we delight in Him, He can trust us with our desires and give them to us without concern that we will use them in ungodly ways. He even shapes them for us and plants many of them within us. He loves to delight those who delight in Him.

I believe the desires God puts in my heart are, like His promises, invitations awaiting a response. I know I have good desires because it's Christ who lives in me, and I have His thoughts and motives in me. So when the Lord says, "He will fulfill the desire of those who fear Him; He also will hear their cry and save them," I can say, "Yes, Lord! Hallelujah!" and know that my desires are lining up with who He is, knowing He wants to fulfill them.

When you realize that, you can speak out the desires in your heart and know that your words are creating something. You can declare all the things you want to see God do in your life, your relationships, your circumstances, and your ministry to other people. I talk about quadriplegics jumping up out of their wheel-chairs, and I get happy about that picture because I know it's going to come to pass. I declare that all my children will love God even more than I do, that my family has favor with God, and that every member is healthy, joyful, and blessed. I say that God gives sleep to His beloved and they wake up happy; that I am prospering and in good health, even as my soul prospers; that I receive fresh revelation and a special treat from the Holy Spirit every time I open the Bible; and that He leads me to banqueting tables that are rich and full of good things for me to eat. All of these are the clearly stated will of God as written in His Word, and they are desires of my heart. I can declare them and believe them with confidence.

I declare words of favor over our network of churches; the lives of our members; the love, joy, and peace of our fellowship; the fruitfulness of our ministries in seeing people saved, healed, and delivered; and on and on. I know many believers who speak these things over their businesses and all their relationships, that they would prosper and demonstrate the fruitfulness, integrity, and excellence of God's character. There is no end to His good-ness, and it applies to every area of our lives. We could really go on and on with all of the great and precious promises and wonderful assurances God gives us in His Word for us to believe and declare.

I can tell you this is working because I have seen it in my life and many others. God is wanting to move His people from head knowledge to heart convictions and real-life application. He has invited us to partake of so much, and as co-heirs of Jesus, in whom all of God's promises are "yes and amen," we should be eager to accept the invitations. We need to move past the days of speaking negatively and discouragingly about ourselves, families, churches, businesses, relationships, communities, leaders, and circumstances because we are often doing more damage to them when our words align with darkness and the enemy's purposes. Don't even honor his work with a conversation about it. When you decide to "just be real," make sure you are being real by God's definition from your position in heaven, not from what your natural eyes see and your anxious and insecure thoughts are telling you. Speak life and hope everywhere you can, and you'll see life and hope coming up all around you.

You can transform your entire family, workplace, or city this way. It doesn't mean you should never acknowledge problems, but so much conversation among believers seems to relish the negative and rejoice in evil. We have no need to slander anyone, and there is always a redemptive, positive, solution-oriented way to talk about the problems and challenges we face. There's no benefit in talking about what doesn't work or what can't be done. We bring answers with the Word of God, revelation and insights from His Spirit, and salvation in His Son.

Jesus never sat around and talked about how horrible the Romans were or how far short God's people had fallen. He didn't gossip about people or talk about how things were falling apart. He did point out the hypocrisy of religious leaders, but He gave them a clear solution. He acknowledged sin and hopelessness, but He offered forgiveness and hope. He confronted death, but He provided a way to overcome it. He spoke words of the kingdom and blessed people with light and life.

That's how you see things change. You can know the Lord has anointed you with the mind of Christ, imparting His desires and motives, downloading ideas and creative solutions into you as you fellowship with Him. Trust the Holy Spirit within you. Declare that you are walking in His wisdom and receiving His creative ideas. Bring your soul into agreement with His purposes and believe His promises. Then you can declare and manifest what you truly believe.

I've declared things that I believed would happen long before there was any evidence of them. I talk about my children with the vision I see for them rather than any troubles or struggles they are currently going through. When I used to drive my daughter in for her exams, we would make declarations all the way there. Having studied hard, she would declare that she communicates well, answers thoroughly and within time limits, has good grades, and has great favor with her professors. And as a result, she would do really well. That's a specific example of the kinds of situations where you can apply your faith through words, but the possibilities are limitless.

You can do this in any area of your life because God wants to accomplish His purposes and plans in your relationships, work, studies, ministry, health, finances, and more. He has called you to share in His anointing as Creator and declare His truth to create and shape the world around you with words. He wants to put His words in your mouth as you partner with Him to bring heaven to earth.

Your Invitation to the Feast

Many Christians are living far below the experience of walking in the reality of what God has promised. If that's true for you, bring your mind, heart, words, and actions into alignment with what He is saying. He is waiting for you to get up and eat from this banqueting table. He doesn't want you to just admire it and talk about it. He wants you to feast.

Long before I was ever pastoring a church, I would talk about our amazingly creative media team who loved working for the ministry and multiplying its influence all over the world. I spoke over my staff before I even had a forum where staff might be needed and declared how dedicated and excellent they were. I talked about my best-selling books before I'd ever written a page, declared a network of churches when there was only one, and claimed fruitfulness in countries I had never been to. I can tell you that when God puts vision into you and you speak it out, things happen.

Faith pleases God. The reluctance to partake of the divine nature—perhaps because you don't think you're deserving or don't want to be greedy—is not appropriate when He has laid it out in front of you and invited you to come. He has actually given you everything you need to come, receive, and be able to represent Him well. If you think you are inadequate, selfish, proud, or not able to make good decisions, you will probably live that out. But if you remind yourself of the truth—that you have been given access to the kingdom of God, and the just live by faith in who Jesus is for them and in them—you can enter into, enjoy, and manifest a new spiritual reality. You can walk right into the throne room of God as His child, not a pauper or victim, and bring your requests boldly to Him. You can declare what He says with holy confidence that you are speaking the will of the Most High God.

CHAPTER 10

Making Room for His Glory

I had an encounter with God in the mid-1990s. It was during that time when the Holy Spirit was being poured out in a new way, and some people were experiencing Him by laughing and shaking and manifesting in all sorts of ways. I didn't know what to think of that at the time, and I thought some people were being a little disrespectful with all their laughing. They actually kind of annoyed me with their behavior during altar calls because I thought they weren't seeking God seriously enough. But I was really hungry for God and wanted whatever He had for me, so I kept going to these meetings where He seemed to be working but also seemed to have a lot of strange things happening.

One night, the Holy Spirit touched me so powerfully that I ended up on the floor and couldn't stop laughing. While I was lying there, I turned my head and had a vision of Jesus. He was looking at me with soft eyes, utterly in love with me. I didn't know how to cope with that. He just looked so in love, gazing at me with those eyes that seemed to look straight into my soul. It was overwhelming.

There's a beautiful prayer at the end of Ephesians 3, where Paul prays that the believers in Ephesus would be strengthened with might in their inner being so they would be able to comprehend Christ dwelling in their hearts through faith and know the love of God that is beyond human understanding (Eph. 3:16-19). In other words, he knew they needed supernatural help to be able to handle how much the Father loved them. Once we begin to taste that love and see those adoring eyes, we need supernatural strength not to turn away. It's just so much. Yet God says He wants to fill us to overflowing with all of His fullness—to enable us to grasp the height, depth, width, and breadth of the love of Christ. It's beyond our ability to comprehend, and it's glorious.

God doesn't want us to settle for just a little taste of that love. He wants us to experience the fullness of it. He invites us to press in, go deeper, and seek more.

Being overwhelmed by a just a look from His eyes, I've wondered what it was like for John when he had a vision of Jesus on the island of Patmos. I've had many profound encounters and experiences with the Lord over the years, but John saw Jesus in His glory—hair white like wool, eyes like flames of fire, His voice like the sound of many waters. It had to have been an astonishing vision, and by John's own account he fell at Jesus' feet "as though dead" (Rev. 1:17). But he was invited to "come up here" to see even more (Rev. 4:1). God wants us to have more and more revelation of who He is.

Recognizing When to Turn Aside

It's important to learn how to steward revelation from God and supernatural experiences. If we don't make room for Him, we risk missing what He wants to show us. Signs and wonders increase when we steward them well, but we experience them less when we don't take time to turn aside, press in, or respond to His invitations.

Moses was tending flocks in the desert when God appeared to him in the flames of a bush that was burning without being consumed (Exod. 3). When he saw the bush, he didn't run home to tell everyone about this amazing phenomenon. He didn't start declaring supernatural signs and wonders to the world. He turned aside to see it. He sensed something supernatural and gave it his full attention. And by making room for that encounter, he heard God speak and commission him to deliver His people out of Egypt.

Two women once went to D.L. Moody, the great evangelist from the late nineteenth century, and told him they had been praying for him to receive the baptism of the Holy Spirit. Even though he already had a large church and had seen people saved through his preaching, he hungered for a baptism of Holy Spirit power, so he told them to keep praying. One day he was walking in New York, preparing to travel to preach in England, and he felt the Holy Spirit moving on his heart. He had a few hours before his ship left, so he went to a friend's house and asked if he could borrow a room to spend some time listening to God. In that room, the power came upon him and he was filled with overwhelming joy.

He later wrote that from that day forward, he was preaching the same sermons the same way he had always preached, yet hundreds at a time were getting saved. But that might not have happened if he hadn't taken the time to turn aside and respond to what God was doing in him. He could have kept walking down the streets of New York, but this nudge from the Holy Spirit prompted him to make room for God. The course of his life—and the lives of many others—was changed in that encounter.

For me, it sometimes feels like a song is rolling around in my heart, and instead of thinking that my mind thought of a certain old song for some inexplicable reason, I've learned to recognize that as an invitation to spend some time worshiping the Lord and going deeper into His presence. I've had to learn to pay attention to those moments and see them as an opportunity to press in a little more or make room to see what He wants to do. He prompts people in different ways—maybe a sensation like with Moody, a song as with me, or just a thought that seems random but isn't— and if you get alone with Him to read the Bible or worship, you might find something waiting for you that is much sweeter and bigger than you had imagined.

When Moses saw the burning bush, he had probably started that day like every other day and assumed there was nothing unusual about it. D.L. Moody was walking the streets of New York on his way to a departure for England, expecting his travels to be the only eventful occasion on that day. But when you make room for God, He often does something dramatic and life-altering. A little bit of time gives Him an opportunity to come in and encounter us in ways that would not happen if we simply remained busy with whatever we were doing. Moses' encounter with God set the course of Israel's destiny. Moody's baptism with the fire and power of the Holy Spirit brought hundreds of thousands more into the kingdom and changed the course of his ministry and many lives. God plans moments for you that will be deeper and richer than you've ever imagined or understood if you take time to make room for Him.

Not every encounter is about changing history, although it very often ends up that way. God enjoys the sound of your voice and the pleasure of your company. I find that amazing. I was once worshiping God and singing to Him, and that night I had a vision of myself giving Him a gift. I asked the Lord what this gift was. What could I possibly have to offer Him? And He said, "Your song is a gift to Me." As I thought about that, I realized I could relate. As a parent, I enjoy watching my kids play and laugh and sing, and when one of my children would say something spontaneous that was full of love for me, it just doesn't get any better than that. That's God's heart for us—the heart of a Father who delights in His children.

Sometimes when we come to God and tell Him we love Him, He responds by opening the door even wider. If we ask Him to set us free from a particular fear, He says, "I'd love to," and comes in to take care of a lot of other fears that are at the root of the problem. He so longs to fill our lives that when we invite Him in and actually make room, create space, and allow time for Him to do something, He gives us even more than we asked.

His Passionate Gaze

Unfortunately, this kind of invitation stirs up guilt in some people. *Yes, I should be making more room for Him in my life,* they tell themselves. *I'll try harder.* And behind those thoughts is the idea that whatever they do to seek God, it won't ever be enough—that they don't have much hope for an encounter with Him because they haven't been doing enough to make Him happy. They assume those encounters are only for the spiritually elite.

But this is not God's perspective at all. That's just buying into the old lie that our old nature is still alive and trying to measure up, not that we reckon ourselves dead to the old life and alive to the new in Christ. When you lift your eyes to the Father, as Jesus lifted His eyes to heaven, God does not look back at you with judgment. He's not thinking, *We'll see about this. That one isn't always serious about these things. I'm not sure how long he/she will pray this time or how much passion is really in that worship. I noticed a bit of mind-wandering last time.* No! When you look to Him in faith, His heart is filled with delight and infinite love for you.

When we start to have faith in who God is, we will no longer be limited by the shame and condemnation that so often makes us give up before we start. Many believers, and really even many segments of the church historically, have been limited for years because they have believed a lie about God. At times, the church has taught that He is an angry God ready to explode with lightning and thunder when people offend Him too directly, or that He is hard to please and too holy for human beings to approach. The truth is that He loves to see your face. It's beautiful to Him, and your voice is sweet to His ears. He delights in His children and opens His arms wide.

God's invitation is like the words of the Bridegroom in the Song of Solomon:

*Can you not discern this new day of destiny breaking
forth around you?*

*The early signs of my purposes and plans are bursting
forth.*

*The budding vines of new life are now blooming
everywhere.*

*The fragrance of their flowers whispers, "There is change
in the air."*

*Arise, my love, my beautiful companion, and run with
me to the higher place.*

For now is the time to arise and come away with me.

For you are my dove, hidden in the split-open rock.

*It was I who took you and hid you up high in the secret
stairway of the sky.*

Let me see your radiant face and hear your sweet voice.

*How beautiful your eyes of worship and lovely your voice
in prayer* (Song of Songs 2:13-14 TPT).

When God looks at you, He is undone. I was undone when
I saw the way He looked at me. But He is undone every time we
come to Him and say, "I'm here, Lord. I love You, Lord." He doesn't
react in judgment to tell us we have no business being there. He
isn't waiting to see if we're sincere enough. He isn't an emotion-
less Father concerned more with discipline and works than with
heartfelt connection. He invented emotions, after all. We are very
emotional creatures made in His image. So He is full of love and
affection for His children. When you speak to Him, you have His
full attention.

God's gaze may be so penetrating, so full of overwhelming love, that you need His strength to be able to handle it. But as you recognize the complete acceptance in His heart and continue to look into His eyes, your confidence grows. You realize you can boldly approach the throne of grace. He has welcomed you into His throne room with open arms.

There may still be some things that hinder the relationship, but His judgment isn't one of them. That was taken care of at the cross. You are alive to God in Christ, fully cleansed and pure, made righteous and holy, with nothing standing between you and your Father's embrace. The only things that can get in the way are the fears, shame, guilt, and distorted perceptions of who He is and how He relates to us.

The imagery in the Song captures this well. Immediately following the beautiful words of the Bridegroom we just read, He adds this:

> You must catch the troubling foxes, those sly little foxes that hinder our relationship.
> For they raid our budding vineyard of love to ruin what I've planted within you.
> Will you catch them and remove them for me? We will do it together (Song of Songs 2:15 TPT).

The little foxes are ruining the vineyard where the bride and the Bridegroom embrace. They spoil the purity of their love. There's no condemnation in that statement, only a plea to catch them together so love can be fully and freely expressed. That's the heart of God for us—not for us to hide our faces in shame and pull away from Him, and not the things that create fear and condemnation in our lives. Perfect love casts out fear (1 John 4:18), and God loves each of us perfectly. He has no intention of provoking guilt in our hearts. He simply wants to identify the "little foxes" in our lives—all of that shame, guilt, condemnation, fear, regret, and emotional distance—so that with His help we can catch them and get them out of the way.

This is where the divine exchange table comes back into the relationship. We catch the little foxes and exchange them for our Beloved's mercy and freedom. The joy of the Lord will fill our hearts because there is absolute joy in His presence (Ps. 16:11). There is no room for anything else but joy. We've given Him everything that could cause us any pain, shame, regret, disgrace, dishonor, condemnation, fear, anxiety, dread, or insecurity. In return, we've received joy, peace, love, righteousness, delight, praise, and beauty—a vineyard free of little foxes that spoil the vine. No more disturbing, distorting emotions to interfere with our love; no more intrusive thoughts to occupy space in our heads that would be much better filled with worship, praise, and gratitude. No more worries and regrets about all the years the locusts have eaten or all the threats that might come against us. We are completely, forever free to love and be loved.

This is where that beautiful, glorious exchange we've been talking about finally leads us. It's not just a restoration; it's a romance. We end up in the arms of the Beloved, His piercing gaze adoring every corner of our souls, with nothing in the way.

Foxes and Foreign Currency

Why would we live with anything less than this? If that is the invitation that is awaiting our response, why would we not respond? When we realize the heart of God and His overwhelming love for us and recognize that we can actually experience Him not as a theory or theology but in real, daily life, we become eager to get rid of the little foxes. We recognize what's at stake in handing over our guilt and shame, those disturbing and distracting thoughts that create distance between us.

And it's very easy to do. We simply say, "Lord, I know these thoughts are wrong, and I don't want them anymore. I cut off the things that create shame in me and turn to You. Thank You for forgiveness. Thank You for removing sin from me as far as the east is from the west. Thank You for the life of Jesus that is now in me. Thank You that I no longer have any need to hang on to regrets, to wish I'd done things differently in the past, to let the guilt and sorrow linger any longer. I am alive to You and walking in a completely new life."

You see, those regrets are like little foxes, and they are very unsettling. They hang around in our minds as "what if" thoughts. *"What if" I had done things differently, not missed those opportunities, made different decisions, stewarded my time better....* But if everything in the past—all the ashes, every sorrow, everything that causes a spirit of heaviness and despair—can be brought to the divine exchange table and exchanged for double blessing now, what is left to regret? Your foreign currency can be redeemed.

All those things that trouble you can be pushed across the table to the Lord, and in return, you can receive forgiveness, mercy, peace, blessing, joy, praise, and freedom. Hallelujah! Receiving double recompense means that your past, as painful as it might be, turns into an asset in the kingdom of God—not simply for what you learned in it, but for what you can receive in its place.

Don't ignore the little foxes that stand in the way of your deep, adoring intimacy with the Lord. Don't just push them down and hope they go away over time. Don't minimize them or pretend they never happened. Bring them boldly to the exchange table and get something for them by faith.

Every distracting, distorting, foreign thought you have can become a prompt for prayer. We are told to be anxious for nothing, but in everything, with prayer and supplication with thanksgiving, to make our requests known to God. Then the peace of God will guard our hearts and minds (Phil. 4:6-7). So we can catch every troubling thought that is rolling around in our minds, give it to God, ask Him to make a miracle out of whatever mess that thought was focused on, and expect a divine exchange—the miracle for the mess. That puts an end to tormenting regrets and paralyzing fears. It sweeps away the ashes and replaces them with beauty, removes sorrow and replaces it with joy, and strips away heaviness so we can be clothed in a garment of praise. It's a wonderful gift.

This is not a one-time deal. Anytime you slip up in the future, you can immediately ask forgiveness and take it to the divine exchange table. Any new thought that provokes worries, fears, regrets, or insecurities can be given directly to Him. It will require some honesty and confession—we tell Him we are sorry for whatever the sin or distorted thought was about—but He is faithful and just to forgive our sins and cleanse us of all unrighteousness (1 John 1:9). Everything that is foreign to the kingdom works as foreign currency, and He knows just what to do with it. And He is ready to bless us with kingdom currency in return.

In light of everything God has promised, we have no reason not to live in freedom and peace. Those thoughts that come in during the night as worries, those regrets that pop up in the middle of the day, those anxieties that seem to keep us captive and provoke responses of fear—all of it is dealt with. That's why we can be told not to be anxious for *anything*. It isn't that there are no more problems in the world or in our lives. It's that God has made a way to exchange everything for our good. And if we ever need help dealing with the little foxes or recognizing the foreign currency still weighing us down, all we have to do is ask. He is so generous and kind, always willing to give us awareness, solutions, ideas, and whatever else we need to capture those foxes and get them out of the vineyard.

If you will recognize these things when they come up, push them across the exchange table, and receive God's double recompense in return, you will be making room for Him in your spirit, mind, and heart. When you become aware of a troublesome thought the looks or smells like pain, shame, or disgrace, you can take it captive and exchange it for perfect peace, supernatural wisdom, and divine solutions. When you recognize a lifestyle habit that is stealing your time with God or inconsistent with His character, you can quickly ask forgiveness and turn it over to Him. It will open up your life to the wisdom, power, and overwhelming love He wants you to experience in Him.

I'm not suggesting a legalistic lifestyle. I'm suggesting a laid-down lifestyle that willingly surrenders. I've lived through an era of religiosity that is based on legalism, and there's no life in it. I did my best to live by an abundance of rules, but I wasn't living from an overflow of revelation of God's goodness and His love for me. I was trying to please Him, fully unaware that He was already pleased. There are still things we should and shouldn't do, but motivation matters. When we do them from a relationship of love, they bring life.

For example, when I was a music teacher, I would often walk around with the last song I heard rolling around in my mind. I used to try to focus on spiritual songs instead because I felt that I should. But now it isn't a matter of what I should do. I don't even want some secular songs in my head because I would rather have my mind filled with things that are holy, pure, and of a good report. It's not a "have to" in order to please Him, it's a desire because I know He is already pleased with me. When you begin to make room for God, you actually want to lay down things that are no longer edifying. You want your thoughts and dreams to be filled with Jesus. You don't do or resist things to cultivate the relationship. The relationship is already there, and what you do flows out of it.

Falling Deeper in Love

When you fall in love with God, you fall in love with what He says. Every word from His heart becomes important to you. And as you intentionally meditate on His Word, memorize it, and talk about it, you are strengthened, built up in faith, and always drawing closer to Him.

Our family has been doing that together for a while now, and as we chew on the Word it's really encouraging and edifying us. We are making room for God, allowing Him to fill our hearts. My daughter Emily and I have been going through some Old Testament books in the mornings, but my son Joseph isn't up quite as early as we are. So when he joins in, we give him a rundown of the passages we've already read. Hearing Emily summarize what she's learned is really quite glorious, and we're all very eager to hear what's next. Sometimes we'll be walking around the mall discussing memory verses, and my children are very careful about making sure they're remembering the right words. We're falling more deeply in love with His Word.

God wants to minister to you through His Word, not as something to add to your to-do list but in order to release fresh revelation and insight. Jesus said, "This is eternal life, that they may know You, the only true God, and Jesus Christ whom You have sent" (John 17:3). Meditating on His Word and being in conversation with Him about it is one way to catch the little foxes, take them to His exchange table, and receive the warmth and blessing of His magnificent love into your heart.

It's fine to watch something on TV in the evenings as you unwind from the day—we're completely free to do things like that because we aren't living according to a list of "shoulds" and "should nots." But we're also free to make other choices sometimes, and the opportunity we have in turning aside to make room for Him could be life changing. Instead of going to bed thinking about the plot of a movie, we'll be thinking about a promise He's planted in our hearts or a revival He wants to bring about in our city. I believe He is offering things we often miss because we're caught up in our routines. But God changed history by interrupting the routines of Moses, D.L. Moody, and many others who have turned aside and made room for the extraordinary. He wants to minister to us far more than we want to minister to Him, and when we give Him just a bit, He very often comes in to overwhelm with His wisdom, power, and love.

I had an experience like that recently. I was at a conference and was invited into the green room, where I met with Michael Brown, who had been part of the leadership at the Pensacola revival years ago. I asked if he would pray for an impartation for revival for me. As he prayed for me and our church's ministry, he began to prophesy Aaron's blessing: "The Lord bless you and keep you; the Lord make His face shine upon you, and be gracious to you; the Lord lift up His countenance upon you, and give you peace." As he prayed, the Holy Spirit unexpectedly came crashing into the room. I began to sob. I couldn't go to sleep that night because I was shaking under the power of God. It surprised me because impartations aren't always like that, but it was very clear that God had released something. When you make a little bit of room—in this case, just a prayer from someone who had an anointing for revival—God can do a lot with it.

Turning aside and making room is not about the physical act of a hand being laid on you, a prayer being spoken, or checking some time you spend reading the Bible off of a to-do list. It's about the expectation of faith that something is going to happen. When you live with expectation, you are hungry for God to set you on fire, revive your heart, and bring His overflow into your life. You begin to anticipate drawing close to Him and receiving from Him. Then when someone lays hands on you or prays a prayer over you, your faith gets released and you receive what you are believing for—and sometimes a lot more.

I've known people who have received very dramatic impartations. I remember when Randy Clark laid hands on me several years ago, I lay on the platform for about 20 minutes, and no one would move me because they could see the Holy Spirit was doing something. Things in my ministry began to explode right after that. But I've also heard of impartations that seemed very uneventful. Bill Johnson says he felt nothing when he went to Toronto to receive an impartation, but as he lay in his bed that night, the Holy Spirit suddenly hit him and he shook all night long. After that, Bethel's ministry began to explode.

My point is that making room for the glory of God is not going to look the same for everyone. For some, it's an instant manifestation. For others, they take it by faith and it manifests later, sometimes suddenly and dramatically and sometimes with things growing and changing supernaturally over time. The issue is not whether you fall, shake, and cry out; it's what you do with what you receive.

Receiving an impartation of glory, a baptism of the Holy Spirit, or for revival is not about a one-off encounter with God. It's about opening ourselves up for the greater measure—not only the double blessing but the multiplied fruitfulness of a relationship with our Beloved. We receive a burning passion to make even more room in our lives for Him.

Revival, both personal and for the church and society as a whole, is a restoration of first things. It involves coming back to our first and truest love. For some, it includes having the scales fall off of their eyes to be able to recognize heavenly realities and the compromises that have robbed the fullness of joy. For others, it is a sudden awareness of the need to repent and no longer live in old patterns of sin, pain, shame, disgrace, or heaviness. The more we see the life of Jesus, the more we realize we don't want anything that doesn't fit with it. The more we want to exchange the old for the new—and recognize that this is an actual promise from God we can enter into. We want to lay down more of ourselves so we can receive and experience more of Him. We make more room for Him because His presence is so much more glorious than we imagined.

Make David's desire your focus:

> *One thing I have desired of the Lord,*
> *That will I seek:*
> *That I may dwell in the house of the Lord*
> *All the days of my life,*
> *To behold the beauty of the Lord,*
> *And to inquire in His temple* (Psalm 27:4).

This is the ultimate restoration. It is infinitely more than double recompense. We bring Him all of our sin, guilt and shame, all of our ashes, sorrows, and heaviness, and we get Him in all of His beauty and glory. Yes, there are blessings involved in that exchange, and they are wonderful to experience. The currency of God's kingdom is so much more liberating and enjoyable

Conclusion

I believe an outpouring of God's Spirit is happening right now. I can sense a revival occurring even in my own heart. God is giving many a fresh awakening. He is pulling many out of a spirit of heaviness and despair and healing all kinds of wounds and regrets with the blessings and benefits of His mercies. He is replacing fears with hopes, problems with promises, and messes with miracles. He is wonderfully kind.

I was recently watching a documentary from almost a decade ago in which I and several other pastors had been interviewed. We were talking about the signs and wonders that were taking place then and the prophecies that had been proclaimed over our nation of Australia and many other parts of the world. As I watched this old footage, my spirit was stirred in a fresh way. I was grateful for all the ways those prayers and prophecies have been fulfilled in the last few years, but I was also hungry for more. And I felt the Holy Spirit ask me if I would still say yes to the call on my life.

He knew I would. Of course I would; why wouldn't I? I said "yes" a long time ago, and I meant it. But it was so kind of Him to remind me of it, now that I know the cost, and still ask me if I say "yes" to more. I want my answer to always be yes to Him.

This is available to all of us. He is doing different things in each of our lives, but they all involve restoration, blessing, an intimate relationship with Him, a zeal for His works and His ways, and a willingness to actively live from our place in heaven toward life on earth rather than the other way around. We bring the blessings of His kingdom into earth because we have experienced them and will continue to do so. We know what His promises mean for us and are committed to applying them to our lives in ever-increasing measure.

That's His will for you. He will keep stirring you to respond to His promptings to turn aside and seek His heart more deeply. He wants you to experience more and more—and to overflow with His goodness for your sake and the sake of those around you. He is not content for any of us to hold on to the pains and troubles of the past. He is always ready at the exchange table, and He is inviting you there every time you find foreign currency weighing you down. He has extended His invitation for you to move from glory to glory. And His invitation is always waiting for your "yes."

About Katherine Ruonala

Senior Leader Glory City Church
Senior Leader, Glory City Network of Churches
Founder and Facilitator of The Australian Prophetic Council

Katherine Ruonala has a prophetic and healing ministry and travels internationally as a conference speaker bringing a message of love and hope to the nations. Katherine carries a strong prophetic and miracle anointing with many being instantly healed in her meetings. Reaching across denominational walls, her ministry is also used to spread the fires of revival and ignite a fresh passion in the hearts of believers to go deeper in their relationship with God.

Katherine hosts her own television show, *Katherine Ruonala TV*, and is author of the best-selling books *Living in the Miraculous: How God's Love Is Expressed Through the Supernatural*, *Wilderness to Wonders: Embracing the Power of Process*, and *Life with the Holy Spirit: Enjoying Intimacy with the Spirit of God*.

Katherine's husband Tom Ruonala is an accomplished businessman and serves as the Honorary Consul of Finland in Brisbane. Katherine is the founder and coordinator of the Australian Prophetic Council and has appeared several times on Sid Roth's *It's Supernatural!* television program, CBN, and other premium TV shows across the world. Katherine is also a Bible school graduate and a qualified music and singing teacher.

Katherine and Tom have been married for over 28 years and have three beautiful children—Jessica, Emily, and Joseph.